BACK FROM TH

The Fall & Rise of Yorkshire's Wildlife

Supported by:

Landscape
Conservation
Forum

Sheffield
Hallam
University

Edited by Margaret Atherden, Ian D. Rotherham and Christine Handley

ISBN: 978-1-904098-68-3

Second Edition September 2018

Published by:
Wildtrack Publishing, Venture House,
103 Arundel Street, Sheffield S1 2NT

Front cover: Comma Butterfly © Ian D. Rotherham

Contents

Introduction

The first edition of this book came out in 2013 published by PLACE at York and has been out of print for some time. It is now re-printed by Wildtrack Publishing with some updates and additions. If anything, the theme is now more pertinent and relevant than ever.

Ian D. Rotherham, 2018

From the first edition:

Over the past half-century there have been many changes in the Yorkshire countryside. Deciduous woodlands have been felled and replaced by conifer plantations; wetlands and ponds have been drained; grasslands have been reseeded, and arable fields have been intensively farmed. Our river systems and coastline have also been subjected to increasing pressure and pollution. All these changes have had dramatic effects on Yorkshire's semi-natural habitats and their associated wildlife. Added to these effects, our climate is altering more rapidly than at any time in the last 10,000 years, leading to further challenges for plants and animals. Some have become locally extinct; others have seen declines in their numbers and/or distributions. From polecats to primroses, fish to fulmars, all have been affected to a greater or lesser extent.

However, it is not all bad news. Some species and habitats are recovering, thanks to national and international legislation and the conservation efforts of individuals and organisations. In this book, which developed from a conference held in Sheffield in 2011, we focus on those organisms and habitats which have experienced a fall and subsequent rise in their fortunes. We examine some of Yorkshire's wetlands, woodlands, cornfields and road verges. We consider how birds, mammals, fish and plants have been conserved, with examples drawn from recent research in various parts of the county. We show how, through the efforts of a range of governmental and non-governmental organisations, habitats and species are now being managed to preserve our biodiversity for the future. In this period of rapid environmental change and ever increasing human impact, the success of such conservation initiatives has never been more vital.

We should like to thank both the authors of the chapters that follow and also the wider group of people who brought along displays and contributed to the success of the original conference. We hope that this book will be of interest both to those who took part in the conference and those who were not able to attend. Most of all, we hope that it will encourage people to continue with their conservation efforts to bring Yorkshire's wildlife '**back from the edge**'.

Margaret Atherden
Christine Handley
Ian D. Rotherham

May 2013

Yorkshire's Forgotten Fenland

Ian D. Rotherham
Sheffield Hallam University

Introduction: Water, Water Everywhere …….

In early medieval times, Holderness was described as *'practically an undrained swamp'* and this was **just one outlier of the great Yorkshire fenland. The Northern Fens of Yorkshire and north Lincolnshire** extended across around 3,000 square kilometres or 1,900 square miles of largely flat lowland landscape (about 400,000 large football pitches). Much of this survived relatively intact until perhaps 400 years ago and a significant proportion well into the 1800s. Stand on relatively high ground looking across a lower-lying valley and you see evidence of former wetlands, their progressive loss and ultimate demise. It is still possible to glimpse how this landscape might have looked, perhaps how it functioned, and even of its importance to local communities. View the landscape from the heart of Thorne Moors for example, grossly modified though they are by centuries of peat stripping and drainage, and you feel something of the magnificence of a landscape (or waterscape) of unfettered nature. Horizon to horizon, no sign of human artefact or construction, today this is an unusual or maybe even unique experience in lowland England. Seek out the great floodlands of Wheldrake Ings near York during a winter flood and you have tantalising views of medieval or even primeval wetlands of ancient Yorkshire. Sadly, most have gone and the remains are tattered fragments of once vibrant ecology. The greatest challenge today is to restore and repair what is left and even to help reinvent and re-construct new additions to Yorkshire's Fens. In the uplands of the North Yorks Moors, the Pennines, the Dales, and the Peak District, the story is similar though perhaps less obvious. Drainage, enclosure and 'improvement' have been transformational. Extensive wetlands have either been at worst, entirely removed, or at best, fragmented and dessicated.

The fate of the rivers sits alongside that of the bogs, marshes and fens, as they have been manipulated and constrained and controlled to do Humankind's will. Only at times of catastrophic flooding such as York in 1998 and 2000, do the rivers break out of their artificial channels to once again, albeit temporarily, become the masters of their own horizons. Rivers are straightened and embanked, dredged and drained, culverted concreted and canalised. Whereas bog, marsh and fen were squeezed dry, the rivers were progressively strangled by generations of engineers, charged with bringing order to chaos and productivity and capitalist profit to what was once a common resource. Throughout the area, new canals and drains were cut and embanked. This was to take off the water and to provide effective transport.

Figure 1: A Yorkshire pike

Modern Times

A trip around Yorkshire will reveal a diversity of wet landscapes and wetland features; some natural and many artificial. Natural sites range from the upland Malham Tarn, to the great lowland coastal lake Hornsea Mere. The county also boasts many rather distinctive and sometimes downright peculiar sites such as the lake at Askern near Doncaster. Most obvious to the casual observer are the modern wetlands and water-bodies associated with water supply to industry, to Victorian canals, and for drinking water for towns and cities. Alongside these are great wetland sites derived from abandoned from mineral workings, and that have been both naturally and deliberately flooded. Visit Fairburn Ings RSPB Nature Reserve near Ferrybridge, just off the A1 for example, to see an ancient wetland drained, then re-wetted through mining subsidence, and today managed and extended as a nature reserve. Here in medieval times, there would be vast winter floodlands and extensive summer grazing and meadow. By the nineteenth century came deep-mined mineral coal and the technology of steam power to drain the mineshafts and allow the working of the hidden coal seam. Almost overnight, the surface waters would have shrunk as the pumps ushered the groundwater away. First of all the land would have been only seasonally wet, and then quickly all trace of flooding would have disappeared. Yet in some ways, this was to be only a short respite. Deep mining of mineral coal includes removal of '*over-burden*' or other rock in which the coal is embedded. Brought to the surface, often then with coal fragments and dust too difficult to extract, this material was dumped across the landscape as '*slag heaps*'. The result was that even with some back filling of the cut areas under-ground, the volume of rock was reduced and the land began the slow process of slumping or subsidence. The result at the surface was the reappearance of so-called subsidence flashes often known as '*ings*' or wet fields. By the 1950s, these were beginning to appear across the Yorkshire coalfields and usually in places, which had formerly been medieval wetlands. Over the next twenty or so years many of these sites were '*discovered*' by local birdwatchers to be 'Meccas' for breeding, wintering and migrating birds. It was from these humble origins that some of the more adventurous and exciting contemporary wetland restoration projects began. The Dearne Valley near Barnsley and the Don Valley around Potteric Carr were other locations for such massive fluxes in wetland fortunes.

Figure 2: Large Copper Butterfly – unrecorded but probably present in the pre-drainage Yorkshire Fens

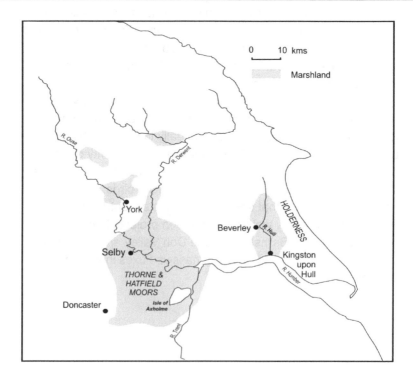

Figure 3: Yorkshire's lowland wetlands before drainage

Other areas such as the lower Swale and Ure valleys in North Yorkshire were the locations for major winning of aggregates, sand and gravels from ancient glacial depositions. Again as the sites have run their commercial course they have been flooded, both accidentally and deliberately, to form sites for water-based recreation and for nature conservation. The Swale and Ure Wetlands now form a sort of miniature '*Norfolk Broads*' of the north with an award-winning restoration and promotional programme. Some locations such as Killamarsh, in the deep south of the county and once mostly in Derbyshire, was historically the biggest wetland in its area, became largely a derelict and despoiled industrial landscape, to then be aggressively opencast for coal in the 1970s, and restored as Rother Valley Country Park. The Upper Dearne Valley north-west of Barnsley came within a whisker of a similar fate but avoided opencast. Wilthorpe Marsh is the final remnant of what must have been a rich and varied valley wetland; but, in the early 1990s, the local farmer and his drainage channels assaulted even this. Over the decades, the same story is repeated with slight local variants across much of the county. The Lower Dearne followed the classic cycle of coal-mining landscapes as described for Fairburn Ings. Here the once great Ferrymoor, with its low-cost Barnsley '*piggy-back ferry*', was a source of food and other materials for local people but was drying up due to mine-water pumping in the mid-1800s. By the early twenty-first century, the process has gone full circle and the RSPB are the now proud managers of a rapidly expanding new wetland landscape.

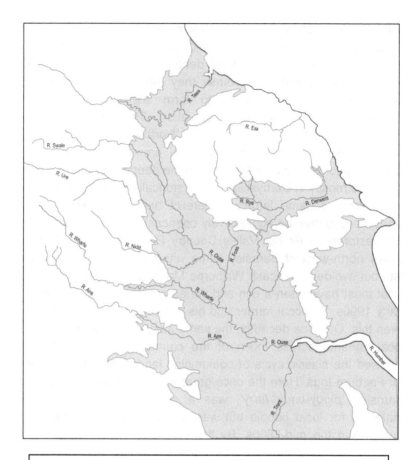

Figure 4: The Yorkshire & North Lincolnshire lowlands

The Former Wetlands and their Fates

So where were the great Yorkshire Fens? Here I need to separate out the uplands from the lowlands, because time and space do not permit me to cover both. As hinted already the uplands to the west of Yorkshire and the great expanse of the North Yorkshire Moors were formerly both much more extensive and indeed a whole lot wetter. The changes influenced the low-lying landscapes in terms of the effects of drainage and desiccation on flooding and on things like habitat continuity and connectivity. Until the 1700s and 1800s, the expanse of vast upland moors and bogs stretched often seamlessly down to the valley and floodplains below. It was only with technologically driven agricultural improvement and massive

8

Victorian urbanisation that these areas became totally separated in both fact and in local perceptions.

However, this story is about '*Yorkshire's Forgotten Fens*', and these are mostly in the lower-lying valleys and in the great floodplains beyond. The medieval fens were dispersed widely across the county and a critical look at landscape and topography helps demonstrate former locations. After agricultural ploughing, the dark organic or paler silt soils can confirm once wetland character. The main areas of lowland wetlands were as follows. There was the vast expanse of the Humberhead Levels in the south and east, the extensive carrs, meres and fens of Holderness, the ancient lake site of the Vale of Pickering, the floodlands of the Vale of York and the Yorkshire Derwent near York, and then lesser but nevertheless significant marshes, fens and washlands along each of the arterial rivers. Some of the former wetlands and their histories are enigmatic and some are totally lost to us. In particular, the Holderness coastline has been rapidly eroding for centuries, at rates of maybe 1-3 metres per year, much more after catastrophic storms. This, and the varying fortunes of saltmarsh and coastal flats around the Humber itself, means that lands have in turn been wetland, reclaimed farmland, and ultimately lost to the sea. Unfortunately, this is a story very often of destruction and irretrievable loss, of human conflict with Nature, and of the long-term consequences of the collective impacts of thousands of individual actions to control and cajole the waters. Much of the loss actually occurred relatively recently, the last century for example, and most happened over the last four hundred years.

A Landscape Transformed

Try to visualise how this wetter landscape might have looked to the medieval peasant or to his landlord. Set in a vast, extensive and expansive lowland landscape would be fens, marshes and seasonal floodlands or washlands. Where acid peat accumulated, would be raised peat bogs covering anything from a few hundred metres to several kilometres. These huge water-absorbing sponges shrank and swelled in the landscape with seasonal rains or droughts. On raised acid sands on glacial materials, there were extensive heaths and grasslands, and there were widespread wet lowland moors too. Across the whole landscape were innumerable smaller ponds and pools with associated stands of marsh and fen. Smaller areas of fen and wet woodland called '*carrs*' dotted the waterscape with Alder (*Alnus glutinosa*) and Willow (*Salix* sp.). The arterial rivers, which permeated this vast morass of wetland, twisted and turned, often back on themselves with meanders and cut-off oxbow lakes; again adding to the diversity and wildlife riches of the area. As people encroached on the largely impenetrable water-world, their early drainage ditches would soon be clogged with rushes and flag, and other weedy vegetation. Gradually rivers were straightened, canals and drains were cut and the tide of water-world was inexorably pushed backwards. Drains and embankments, pumps and sluices gradually exerted human technological and political control over once independent and free waters. By the nineteenth century, engineers and improvers held sway over the formerly independent waterscape. Now in the early twenty-first century, this change has been wrought so effectively and the transformations etched so deeply into the landscape that there is often little recollection that wetland and fluid Nature ever existed. Perhaps the hardest thing is to imagine the wildlife riches of the pristine primeval or the medieval waterscapes across most of lowland Yorkshire. There are few records since almost nobody could write, there were no accepted identification or classification systems, and few people were interested in or able to record and document the ecology. We can get some insight into an amazingly rich natural resource from the account books of houses, halls, and great estates and, where they exist, from the records of hunting and of feasting. There is a final source of information and this relates too to the unique archival record of the peat bogs that remain. Preserved dead remains of plants and animals, embalmed by peat acids and a lack of oxygen, have their secrets revealed by teams of palynologists, palaeo-ecologists and palaeo-archaeologists.

A Wetland Lost From Memory

The Holderness valleys were swathed by fens and carrs which opened into salt marsh and flats along the Humber shoreline; with Kingston-upon-Hull essentially an island surrounded by brackish water and shifting sands. The Julian Dyke and an aqueduct brought supplies of freshwater to the city, but this had collapsed by around 1507 and water had to be brought in by boat. As can be imagined the excessive cost of this operation for such a basic commodity, was a source of much consternation to the inhabitants.

York itself was an island between rivers and swamps. The Vale of York with its underlying clays provided excellent summer pasture and meadow but in winter was awash with floodwaters and described by Smout (2000) as '...*full of meres and flooded in winter .... The Derwent in particular was liable to flood at any time of year*'. Leland in the 1500s described the Derwent as '.... *this river at greate raynes rageth and overflowith*', and Defoe later suggested that it '.... *overflows its banks and all the neighbouring meadows always after rain.*' For modern-day inhabitants of York and the Vale this may sound terribly familiar.

Figure 5: Topographic representation of the regional landscape (courtesy of the Environment Agency)

The waterscape was enigmatic, on the one hand providing sustenance, security and even wealth, but on the other, potentially fearful, destructive and the harbourer of disease. Perhaps even more a reason for its ultimate and almost total destruction was that the Northern Fen was a disputed territory. It granted livelihood and independence to people within and around it. It sometimes generated wealth for landowners too and certainly afforded exotic food for the feast table and sporting opportunities for both aristocrat and crown. Yet it was the desire to bring the waterscape into control, back onto the dry land, and to limit the independence of local people that was the undoing of the Fen. Ultimately, their efforts were harnessed to generate wealth against capital investment for the Church, then the Crown, and eventually for individual landowners and investors. The final stages during the nineteenth and twentieth centuries were paid for largely from the public purse and even by the European Union through agricultural subsidies.

The farmers' fields were thoroughly drained with subsoil trenched, and surrounded by networks of ditches, dykes and surface drains to carry superfluous water away. The fields were uniform, tidied and hedged or walled, and the soils homogenised and manicured. With fertilisers, marl or lime, and ironically in many lowland areas, irrigation, these former waterscapes became the breadbaskets of the country. As if buoyed by the efforts of the farmers, the engineers continued their mission of draining marsh, fen and bog. In Yorkshire, Thomas Allen (1828) was lavish with his praise for the Act of Parliament in 1811, which facilitated a further phase of enclosure and improvement around the once intractable Thorne and Hatfield Moors. He noted how 212,000 acres of the '*wide extent of waste*' was converted into '*waving fields of corn*'. In the East Riding of Yorkshire:

> '*Within the last half century the vast commons of Wallinfen and Bishopsoil, containing upwards of nine thousand acres, have been enclosed and cultivated, besides several others of inferior extent; and a vast or dreary waste, full of swamps and broken grounds, which in foggy or stormy weather could not be crossed without danger, is now*

covered with well-built farm houses and intersected in various directions with roads.'

Figure 6: Yorkshire leech catchers in the early 1800s give a feel of a lost landscape

The Final Nail in the Coffin

The late Victorian period did little to halt the demise of the greater wetlands but it did slow the impact of farmland drainage and its intensification. The coming of steam power and then other modern energy sources facilitated more effective drainage and water management, and across many areas, the industrial revolution took its toll. The *Country Gentleman Magazine* (1894) noted that '…. *there is not time for the land nearly to repay the outlay before it requires draining again'*. This situation continued, on and off, for the next thirty to forty years, through the Depression years until the outbreak of World War Two. During and then after the War, all the land abandoned since the Victorian improvers and more besides was reclaimed for agriculture. The efforts went beyond this, and especially utilising the new technologies of petrol and diesel tractors and tracked vehicles, the farmers and land improvers mopped the remaining sites left undrained by the Victorians. Technological innovations allowed landowners to remove marshes, heaths and fens, and to further drain and improve arable and pasture. Simple innovations such as plastic piping made a difference, as did mechanical draglines and the availability of diesel pumps and then electric pumps. There was still an incentive throughout most of this period for farmers to maintain ponds both on the farm and in the local village. These were necessary for both watering of livestock and for wetting wooden carts and the like. Since the 1950s, there has been a general move towards stock watered by piped water to drinking troughs and ponds either abandoned or infilled. After the 1980s, there has been some limited recovery with the reinstatement of farm conservation ponds.

Figure 7: Peat extraction by horse and waggon

A result of '*improvement*' was widespread uniformity of modern lowland farming landscapes. The pre-improvement landscape was a matrix and mosaic of wet and dry, and of differing vegetation or land-use. By the 1980s, this had totally changed to often-monotonous improved grassland or intensive arable. There was gradually a slowing of government-funded drainage and improvement schemes, but even up to the 1970s, big projects like the reclamation of the Lound and Idle Washlands around Bawtry, in the south of the Humberhead Levels, went ahead. With remaining sites recognised for unique conservation interest, the tide began to turn. Some areas were in part protected as *Sites of Special Scientific Interest* and legislation eventually tightened its grip on these areas. Other sites like Wheldrake Ings were acquired as National Nature Reserves. The Wildlife Trusts and ultimately the RSPB also took on sites as Nature Reserves. Yet more lands along rivers received protection as designated floodlands or washlands to hold excess at times of inundations. Various bodies derived from the old Water Authorities managed these areas. They were briefly the National Rivers Authority, and now the Environment Agency. Surprisingly it is only relatively recently that many of these areas have moved from management for income generation often by itinerant graziers on short-term leases towards more environmentally-positive land-uses. Certainly, by the 1990s, many of the riverside washlands were desperately over-grazed and readily losing biodiversity.

In parallel with the widespread farming 'improvement' described above, there were some other distinctive trends in parts of the Yorkshire region. One of the most significant of these was the impact of peat cutting, which was, by the 1980s and 1990s, a hugely contentious nature conservation issue. By this time, most of the aggressive applications for post-WW2 opencast coal mining had stopped, but colossal damage had been done. The progressive losses were to an extent compensated by industrial and other working water-bodies, such as reservoirs. There also were ornamental lakes and pools of great landscaped parks and gardens of rich and powerful landowners, and later the industrial barons of Yorkshire's towns and cities. Over time during the latter twentieth century, there developed a network of wetland nature reserves, Country Parks, and created wetlands on former industrial lands. Whilst many of these water-bodies are valuable for wildlife, and often for water-based recreation, they are different from the areas lost and less intimately embedded in their landscapes. They are mostly deeper and more stable, and lack the smaller-scale mosaics of habitats and ephemeral waters of the old Yorkshire Fen.

Another major difference between the new and the old is the relationship with local people. For centuries, the Yorkshire Fen was at the heart of its subsistence community and folk made their living and livelihoods in and around the waterscapes. Today when they exist, these are mostly leisure landscapes, ornaments to recreation, or conservation sites. With this change in ownership, purpose and emphasis there come some long-term problems. All these issues and their histories are reflected in the accounts of the Yorkshire regions and their lost wetlands and fens. Each landscape presents a unique sub-plot but in its way contributes to the totality of the wider story. The Yorkshire agricultural writer and improver William Marshall captured the essence of the issue when describing in the late 1700s how:

'In RIVERS, the County under survey is singularly well supplied. The Humber, which might be styled the River of rivers, bonds on the south. The Tees forms its northern confine. The Don, The air, the Wharf, the Ouse, and the Derwent rise in its mountains, and wind through its plains. In commercial light, these rivers are objects of the first magnitude. The tide flows into the center of the county. Not only Hull, but York, Tadcaster, Ferrybridge and Doncaster, may be called inland ports. The Don is rendered navigable, to Rotherham, Sheffield; the Air, to Leeds, Bradford; the Calder, to Wakefield and up to near Halifax; the Ouse, to Burroughbridge; the Derwent, to Malton; the Hull, to Driffield, at the foot of the Wolds; and the Tees, to Yarm, on the borders of Cleveland, at the head of the Vale of York.'

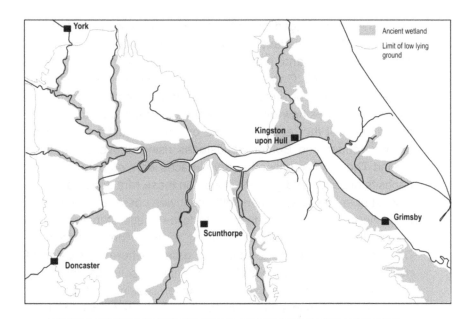

Figure 8: The Humber wetlands and washlands

The Northern Fens of Yorkshire and North Lincolnshire

In the early 1960s, Alice Garnett was one of the first to write of the *'Humber Fen'* and the *'Humber Levels'*. She described how the landscape to the east of the exposed coalfield of South Yorkshire changed markedly after the River Don runs through the Don Gorge for around four miles, cutting through the dramatic 300-400 foot Magnesian Limestone ridge that runs north / south. At the western end is the great Norman Conisbrough Castle; guarding the strategically important point of the river and of route-ways north to south, and east to west. This is the land of Sir Walter Scott and of Ivanhoe. Our wetlands lie east of here where the river opens out into a low, broad plain of the *Humberhead Levels* that remain from the once great proglacial Lake Humber. The land surface is covered by postglacial deposits of drift or mud (boulder clay) and alluvium from early watercourses that meandered across this vast featureless plain in prehistory. The consequences for the landscape which evolved over time until recently, was an expansive, waterlogged or wet area with few obvious features to stand out. Most of the land is or was around twenty-five feet or less above sea level; and much is at or around the contemporary modern sea level. Garnett goes on to describe the remains of ancient peat bogs, now mostly drained, around Thorne and Hatfield Moors. She notes how over long periods of prehistoric and historic times, much of the region was lake or fen, with just a few islands on the Keuper and Bunter Sandstones rising above the fenland around Thorne. The only other dry surfaces were on outwash delta deposits of sands and gravels. It was on these rare zones of dry or at least drier land that human settlement was possible. The Roman Road north from London diverted to follow these stepping-stones across the fen and marsh resulting in the Roman station at Doncaster being on the lowest solid ground where a crossing of river and wetland was possible. The fenland itself was valued by fishermen and fowlers, and by those seeking respite from persecution and sanctuary from the law. In its later periods from Saxon times onwards, much of the region was preserved as a hunting chase.

The great wetland extended beyond the region called the Humberhead Levels today and wider than that used by Garnett in the 1960s. In the north the Fenland extending along the Derwent and Ouse to York, with an outlier beyond in the Vale of Pickering, and up the Hull Valley into Holderness, and in the south it sent fingers of wetland and marsh along the Trent Valley and the Ancholme in north Lincolnshire. Taken together these made up what I describe as the Northern or Yorkshire Fens, and it was not until the drainage schemes of the early seventeenth century that the region's wetland landscape was significantly changed. The works of Vermuyden and his 'Adventurers', and then of those who followed, changed the landscape from a wetland with the Rivers Don, Torne, and Idle meandering over a vast flatland between the great Rivers Ouse and Trent. The Don was diverted north along the new Dutch River to the Ouse confluence at Goole. The Idle and the Torne were taken into new channels to the Trent north of Axholme. Then with pumping by windmills and the practice of warping as described later, the land was transformed into one of productive farmland and dispersed settlements and farmsteads.

Through the 1800s and 1900s there followed further and more effective drainage of the remaining fens and marshes, and the improvement and under-drainage of much of the farmland. This process, as we have seen, continued unabated until the 1990s. By the late twentieth century, even the memories of this once great wetland complex had been erased from both corporate and community mental maps of the region. The Yorkshire Fens have been forgotten but in the light of climate change, flood-risk, and sea level rise, it would be wise to re-kindle our memories of these lost landscapes.

FLOODS SEEN FROM BENTLEY ROAD, DONCASTER MAY 1932

Figure 9: Flooding at Bentley Road Doncaster in May 1932

Bibliography

Burdett (1767) *Map of the County of Derbyshire*. Derbyshire County Libraries, Matlock.

Colbeck, J. (1782) *Plan of the rivers cuts drains and watercourses subject to the direction of the Trustees and which drain and preserve certain Lands within the parishes Townships and Hamlets of Doncaster Balby Carhouse High.*

Dinnin, M. (1997) The drainage history of the Humberhead Levels. In: Van de Noort, R. and Ellis, S. (eds) (1997) *Wetland Heritage of the Humberhead Levels: An Archaeological Survey*. Humber Wetlands project, University of Hull, Hull.

Jeffrys (1772) *Map of the County of Yorkshire*. Harry Margary, Lympne, Kent (1973).

Rotherham, I.D. (ed.) (2008) *Flooding, Water and the Landscape*. Wildtrack Publishing, Sheffield.. 185 pp.

Rotherham, I.D. (2008) Landscape, Water and History. *Practical Ecology and Conservation*, 7, 138-152.

Rotherham, I.D. (2008a) Floods and Water: A Landscape-scale Response. *Practical Ecology and Conservation*, 7, 128-137.

Rotherham, I.D. (2009) *Peat and Peat Cutting*. Shire Publications, Oxford.

Rotherham, I.D. (2010) *Yorkshire's Forgotten Fenlands*. Pen & Sword Books Limited, Barnsley..

Rotherham, I.D. (2013) *The Lost Fens: England's Greatest Ecological Disaster*. The History Press, Stroud.

Rotherham I.D. & Cartwright, G. (2006) *Water and wetlands: their conservation and re-creation in a social landscape – the vital role of project champions*. Proceedings of the IALE Conference, *Water and the Landscape: The Landscape Ecology of Freshwater Ecosystems*, 321-326.

Rotherham, I.D. & Harrison, K. (2006) *History and ecology in the reconstruction of the South Yorkshire fens: past, present and future*. Proceedings of the IALE Conference, *Water and the Landscape: The Landscape Ecology of Freshwater Ecosystems*, 8-16.

Rotherham, I.D. & Harrison, K. (2009) *South Yorkshire Fens Past, Present and Future: Ecology and Economics as Drivers for Re-wilding and Restoration?* In: Hall, M. (ed.) *Greening History: The*

Presence of the Past in Environmental Restoration. Routledge Publishing, London, 143-153.

Rotherham, I.D. & McCallam, D. (2008) *Peat Bogs, Marshes and Fen as disputed Landscapes in Late eighteenth-Century France and England.* Lyle, L. & McCallam, D. (eds) *Histoires de la Terre: Earth Sciences and French Culture 1740-1940.* Rodopi B.V., Amsterdam & New York, 75-90.

Rackham, O. (1986) *The History of the Countryside.* J M Dent & Sons, London.

Saxton, C. (1577) *Map of the County of Yorkshire.*

Saxton C & Goodman W (1616) *Map Of Pottrick Carr near Doncaster.* Local Archives, Doncaster MBC Libraries.

Smout, C. (2000) *Nature Contested - environmental history in Scotland and Northern England since 1600.* Edinburgh University Press, Edinburgh.

Darby, H.C. & Maxwell, I.S. (eds) (1962) *The Domesday Geography of Northern England.* Cambridge University Press, Cambridge.

Van de Noort, R. & Davies, P. (1993) *Wetland Heritage: an archaeological assessment of the Humber Wetlands.* Humber Wetlands project, University of Hull, Hull.

Van de Noort, R. & Ellis, S. (1997) *Wetland Heritage of the Humberhead Levels: An Archaeological Survey.* Humber Wetlands project, University of Hull, Hull.

Skidmore, P., Limbert, M. & Eversham, B.C. (1985) The Insects of Thorne Moors. *Sorby Record* Supplement, **No. 23**,

Vermuyden, C. (1626) *Map of Hatfield Chace Before The Drainage.*

Figure 10: Fenland scene

'Woodman Spare That Tree': The Rescue of South Yorkshire's Ancient Woodlands

Melvyn Jones
Sheffield Hallam University

Introduction

South Yorkshire's ancient woods have great heritage value. It is the inherited characteristics of these ancient woods – their sites, their locations, their shapes, their variety of plant life and the animals that inhabit them, their archaeology, and their often long documented history – that make them so very special. **These woods take us back to the roots of our history and are irreplaceable**.

They have disappeared or have been reduced in size over a long period because of clearance for quarrying and mining operations, through agricultural expansion, industrial development, the spread of settlement and road building. The destruction of the woods at Shirecliffe in Sheffield over more than two centuries illustrates this very clearly. Despite this widespread destruction, it is surprising how many ancient woods have survived across the region. According to the Nature Conservancy Council's woodland inventory (1986) there are 333 ancient woodland sites in South Yorkshire covering nearly 11,000 acres (4,451 ha) or just 2.8 per cent of the land surface. Ancient woodland is unevenly distributed across South Yorkshire, with nearly three-quarters of the surviving sites on the extensive exposed Coal Measures (Figure 1).

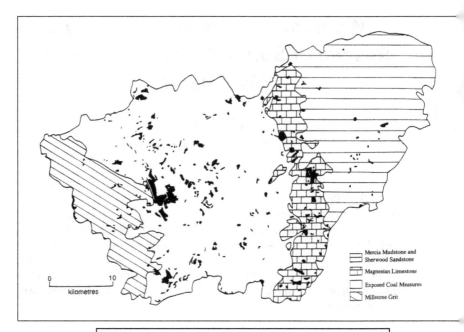

**Figure 1: Ancient woods in South Yorkshire
(Nature Conservancy Council, 1986)**

However the surviving ancient woods, for almost a century until the late 1980s, excepting the minority still in private hands (which were often coniferised), were neglected and unmanaged. Sites became increasingly even-aged with dense canopies and poorly developed shrub layers. They contained much poorer displays of spring flowers, some breeding birds and butterflies had been reduced in number or were no longer found in woods where they were once common, and local residents were increasingly afraid of walking in the woods because they were dark and gloomy. The more accessible woods were also sometimes heavily vandalised and full of litter. After having survived for hundreds, and in some cases for thousands of years, there was a real danger that South Yorkshire's woodland heritage would be squandered.

Thankfully, that phase in their history appears to be drawing to a close, but it has been a long transition from destruction, vandalism and benign neglect to management and protection. To illustrate problems and trends, the main part of the paper will look at episodes in the recent history of three woodland sites. These are the campaign to save Edlington Wood in the 1970s; renewed management since 1988 of Bowden Housteads Wood in Sheffield

24

after a century of neglect; and the purchase in 1988 of Broad Ing Wood at Tankersley from the Forestry Commission and its restoration as a community wood. Finally the importance of the *Fuelling a Revolution* project will be discussed.

The campaign to save Edlington Wood in the 1970s

At the beginning of the 1970s, it looked as if Edlington Wood, the largest ancient wood in the Magnesian Limestone zone, then covering more than 350 acres (142 ha) would become part of the catalogue of recent unprecedented woodland destruction.

The wood contains an upper Palaeolithic/early Mesolithic rock shelter, the remains of Romano-British field systems and a mysterious linear earthwork, the Double Dyke (Figure 2). It is equally important ecologically. In the northern part of the site where the limestone outcrops in natural crags there appears to be natural woodland dominated by small-leaved lime, ash and wych elm together with many ancient yews. The understorey is well developed and contains shrubs typical of limestone such as wild privet, dogwood, spindle, buckthorn and spurge-laurel. There is a diverse ground flora including more than thirty ancient woodland indicators.

Figure 2: Edlington Wood as shown on the First Edition One Inch OS map, 1841

In 1700, as part of the manor of Edlington, it was purchased by Robert Molesworth, MP who later became Viscount Molesworth. After his death the woodland was converted into a coppice-with-standards and then in 1748, when it covered 350 acres (142 ha) it was bought by the first Marquis of Rockingham of Wentworth Woodhouse and added to his already extensive acreage of coppice-with-standards woods. During the nineteenth century, planting took place. At some unknown date, the wood passed into the ownership of the Earls Nelson of Stafford and the Forestry Commission managed it on their behalf until in the spring of 1971 it was sold to another private owner. Anticipating activity on the site that might result in woodland destruction and affect public access, Doncaster Rural District Council protected the wood by means of a Tree Preservation Order (TPO). In September 1971, the new owner went public with his intentions for the site. These included quarrying and clearance for agriculture and house building. His proposals were met with much local opposition and anger and an action committee was set up to oppose them. There then followed several years of applications from the owner to clear part of the woodland, to introduce quarrying on the site and to fell and to thin. In spite of the TPO the new owner pressed on with his plans. In November 1971, it was learned that planning permission had been given to clear sixty acres in the wood for agriculture that the owner claimed contained no mature trees (and was not covered by the TPO). The action committee arranged meetings with the local MP and the Minister for the Environment, members of the West Riding Council and the Forestry Commission, but the decision was not changed. Activity by the owner did not stop there. In January 1972, it was learned that felling operations were taking place in those parts of the wood covered by the TPO. Doncaster Rural District Council decided to prosecute and the owner was taken to court and fined. He then applied to open quarries in the wood and to carry out thinning operations. The campaigners were joined in their opposition to the proposed quarrying by the Rural District Council and the Planning Committee strongly recommended refusal. The proposed thinning operations initially received the support of the West Riding County Council but after a year of protest meetings, reports and the support of professional ecologists permission was refused. In November 1973 a group of local and regional specialists in history, archaeology, geology and natural history compiled a 237-page book about the wood, *Edlington Wood*, printed by Doncaster Rural District Council, to further try to convince the owner and the authorities of the importance of the site and the need to protect it.

Problems and protests rumbled on through the 1970s until in 1979 most of the wood (247 acres (100 ha)) was provided with legal protection by being given the status of a Site of Special Scientific Interest (SSSI) by the then Nature Conservancy Council (now Natural England).

Renewed management of Bowden Housteads Wood after a century of neglect

Bowden Housteads is one of the earliest recorded ancient woods in South Yorkshire, being recorded as early as 1332 as a wood pasture. By 1600 it was a coppice-with-standards and was coppiced continuously until almost the end of the nineteenth century. It was heavily planted in the late nineteenth century. In 1916, the Duke of Norfolk sold the wood to Sheffield Corporation for £6,000 for use as a place of recreation. Since then, not only was it left virtually unmanaged for more than 70 years, but also a section of the wood was lost through opencast coal mining in the 1940s. It was also bisected by the construction of the Sheffield Parkway (A630) in 1970 and the southern part of the wood was further sub-divided by the creation of the Mosborough Parkway in 1990 (Figure 3). The wood became increasingly even-aged, with a dense canopy resulting from the closely-planted trees, especially in those areas dominated by beech, causing suppression of ground flora and erosion of bare soils on steep slopes. However, it was still a heavily used public open space. (The detailed history of the site's management and related issues are described by Rotherham & Jones, 2011, and Jones & Rotherham, 2012)

Sheffield City Council's Recreation Department created a 'Moorland and Amenity Woodland Advisory Group' (MAWAG) in the 1970s made up of council officers and representatives of environmental organisations. The City Council then approved a Woodland Policy, put together by MAWAG, in 1987. The Woodland Policy was put into action in Bowden Housteads Wood in the early spring of 1988, the project being funded jointly by the City Council and the Countryside Commission.

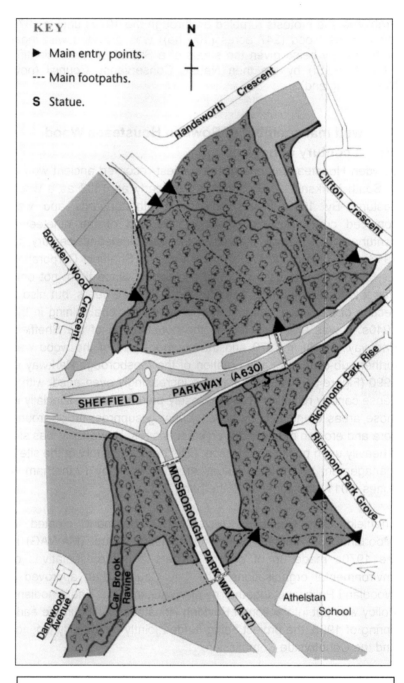

KEY

▶ Main entry points.

--- Main footpaths.

S Statue.

Figure 3: Bowden Housteads Wood

Figure 4: Stream-side glade in Bowden Housteads Wood

The main operation was thinning, to provide more space for the native trees to develop, and to help diversify the woodland by encouraging the regeneration of the shrub layer and the flowering of the ground flora. The thinning was irregular and several glades were created (Figure 4).

A second management plan for Bowden Housteads, to build on the work undertaken between 1987 and 1991, was compiled, covering the period from 2000 to 2005. The vegetation management objectives of the plan were to restore natural species composition by continued selective thinning of sycamore, whitebeam and beech and so encouraging natural regeneration. Willow would be encouraged in selected wet areas and the age diversity of the woodland would be further encouraged through the reintroduction of group felling. The most recent plan published for the wood covers the period 2009-2013 and aims to build on the work undertaken as part of the plans for 1987-1991 and 2000-2005.

The purchase of Broad Ing Plantation from the Forestry Commission by Tankersley Parish Council

Two hundred years ago the site was partly wooded (called Broad Ing Bushes) and partly farmland. In the early nineteenth century both the scrub woodland and the meadow became an ironstone mining area, mostly in the form of bell pit mining. After ironstone mining ceased the area was made into a plantation that was felled and replanted on a number of occasions. In 1987, when its purchase was being contemplated by the local parish council, Broad Ing Plantation was a small (10-acre (4-ha)) Forestry Commission plantation, managed purely for economic reasons. It had been restocked in 1964 with sycamore (covering just over half of the plantation) and Japanese larch.

In December 1988, the purchase was completed and the following spring, work started on the first five-year management plan. The plan contained a prescription covering the short term, medium-term and long-term objectives. Short-term objectives included thinning 25-30 per cent of the larch and sycamore to encourage a more diverse woodland environment, removing bramble infestation, leaving part of the wood in which planting had been ineffective as a non-intervention area, undertaking some judicial planting of hawthorn, holly and hazel, creating a glade where the ground flora was richest to encourage further spread and flowering, leaving dead and dying timber and some felled timber to rot, and creating piles of brushwood to provide shelter and nesting sites. The long-term objective was to arrive at naturally-regenerating native woodland through continued periodic thinning until all of the larch and most of the sycamores had been removed. The main features of the proposed management are shown in Figure 5. A second detailed management plan covering the period 1999-2003 was compiled which, with support from the Forestry Commission's Woodland Grant Scheme (WGS), enabled the thinning operations, planting and improvement and maintenance of the footpath system to continue.

Fuelling a Revolution Project

A major influence on local attitudes to woodland management in the last two decades was been the **South Yorkshire Forest Project** (later **Partnership**). This project, established in 1991, was a partnership between Barnsley, Rotherham and Sheffield Councils, the Countryside Agency and the Forestry Commission. Its aim is to develop multipurpose forests, which will create better environments for people to use, cherish and enjoy. The *South Yorkshire Forest* area covers most of the Coal Measure country in the three metropolitan districts. In 1997, the South Yorkshire Forest Team put together a £1½ m bid to the Heritage Lottery Fund for a five-year action plan to restore 35 Coal Measure woodlands in Sheffield, Rotherham and Barnsley – called *Fuelling a Revolution - The Woods that Founded the Steel Country.* In February 1999 it was announced that the bid had been successful and a five-year Heritage Woodlands Project was launched in September 1999. The project also helped Rotherham MBC buy Canklow Wood from the Duke of Norfolk for £135,000, £101,000 of which was provided by the Heritage Lottery Fund. There has been much activity on a broad front connected with the project – archaeological surveys, development of management plans, active woodland management programmes (Figure 6), interpretation for local communities, the development of educational materials and activities and the commissioning of public art works. [Due to government budget cuts the South Yorkshire Forest Partnership closed in 2016. Ed. 2018]

The future of South Yorkshire's woodlands looks much better now than it did three decades ago. Awareness of the cultural importance of ancient woods has been raised to a much higher level than hitherto and interest in their critical importance for wildlife as well as their educational and recreational potential has been re-awakened. Important players have not only been the local authorities, the South Yorkshire Forest Partnership and the Heritage Lottery Fund but also the Woodland Trust, special interest groups such as the many 'Friends of' groups, The Working Woodland Trust and the South Yorkshire Biodiversity Research Group. **But it cannot be emphasised enough that woodland management is not a one-off event; it needs to be continuous and long-term. The work that has recently taken place is very encouraging, but it is just the beginning; the challenge is to sustain it in the medium and long term. [The closure of South Yorkshire Forest and cuts to local authority services and government conservation agencies are reasons for long-term concern. Ed, 2018)**

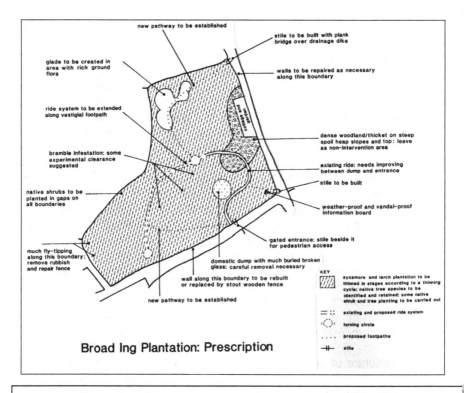

Broad Ing Plantation: Prescription

Figure 5: Management prescription for Broad Ing Plantation, 1989

Figure 6: 'Snagging in Woolley Wood

Further Reading

Jones, M. (1988) *Broad Ing Plantation: survey and management plan*. For Tankersley Parish Council, Barnsley.

Jones, M. (1998) The Coal Measure Woodlands of South Yorkshire: Past, Present and Future in M.A. Atherden and R.A. Butlin (eds) *Woodland in the Landscape: Past and Future Perspectives*, PLACE Research Centre, pp.79-102.

Jones, M. (2009) *Sheffield's Woodland Heritage*, 4th edition, Wildtrack Publishing, Sheffield.

Jones, M. & Rotherham, I.D. (2012) Managing urban ancient woodlands: a case study of Bowden Housteads Wood, Sheffield. *Arboricultural Journal*, **34** (3), 215-233.

Phillips, H. (ed) (1973) *Edlington Wood*, Doncaster Rural District Council.

Rotherham, I.D. & Jones, M. (2011) Management issues in urban ancient woodlands; a case study of Bowden Housteads Wood, Sheffield. *Aspects of Applied Biology*, **108**, 113-121.

Rotherham, I.D., Jones, M., Smith, L. and Handley, C. (2008) (eds) *The Woodland Heritage Manual: A Guide to Investigating Wooded Landscapes*, Wildtrack Publishing.

Sheffield City Council (1987) *Bowden Housteads / Corker Bottoms 'Greenlink' Management Plan*, Department of Land and Planning, Sheffield City Council, Sheffield.

Sheffield City Council (2000) *Bowden Housteads and Spring Wood, Management Plan 2000-2005*, Leisure Services, Parks, Woodlands and Countryside, Sheffield City Council, Sheffield.

Sheffield City Council (2009) *Bowden Housteads Wood Draft Management Plan 2009-2013*, Directorate of Place, Parks and Countryside, Sheffield City Council, Sheffield

South Yorkshire Forest (1997) *Fuelling a Revolution – the Woods that Founded the Steel Country, application to the Heritage Lottery Fund (No 96-00700).*

Tankersley Parish Council (1999) *Broad Ing Plantation Management Plan.* Tankersley Parish Council, Barnsley.

Dial 'P' for Polecat:
The return of the Polecat Mustela putorius to Yorkshire

Colin A. Howes
YNU Mammal Recorder

Historical status and distribution changes of the Polecat in Yorkshire

Archival and literature searches provided evidence of past abundance, widespread distribution and subsequent decline and extinction of the polecat *Musela putorius* L. in Yorkshire and adjacent counties (Howes, 1980, 1985c, 2009). Here, various forms of land-use changes and intra-guild interactions are reviewed as possible causes of the polecat's decline.

Of 157 sets of Yorkshire parish records from 1619 to 1837 examined by Howes (1980a, 2009) and Lovegrove (2007), 102 include head money for carnivores. Of 10,584 records 5,545 (52% of all carnivore records) were creatures deemed to be polecat (*M. putorius*), usually referred to under various versions of the terms foulmart or foumar.

Historical distribution

By plotting the locations of parishes where polecat bounty payments were made from the seventeenth to the nineteenth centuries and adding in records from literature references of the nineteenth and early twentieth centuries, Figure 1 shows its former distribution throughout Watsonian Yorkshire.

Evidence of status changes

Langley & Yalden (1977) elegantly illustrated the progressive diminution of range and final extinction of polecat (and other rare carnivore) populations, from 1800 to 1915. The primary cause of the decline deemed to be persecution by gamekeepers.

The analysis of Yorkshire parish vermin bounty records (Howes, 1980 and 2009) indicates that the decline had actually been in progress long before the advent of shooting estates and the battalions of gamekeepers, and that other factors were clearly involved in this decline. This population crash is illustrated by plotting the highest annual number of polecat bounties per parish per decade against the acreages of the parishes concerned and the results expressed as bounties per 100 acres per decade. Figure 2 shows a significant and progressive decline in polecat density from the mid-seventeenth century to the mid-nineteenth century.

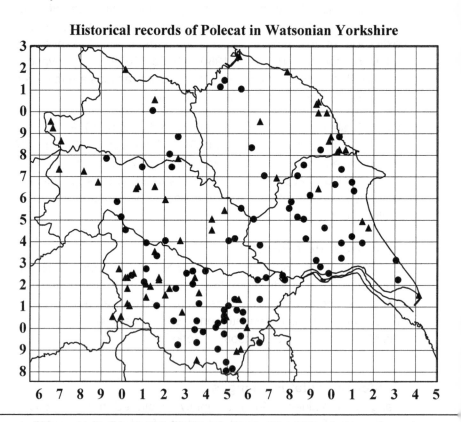

Historical records of Polecat in Watsonian Yorkshire

Figure 1. Polecat distribution in Yorkshire based on • = bounty payments in Parish and Township accounts from the seventeenth to the nineteenth centuries and ▲ = Literature references from the nineteenth to the early twentieth centuries (from Howes 1980 & 2009)

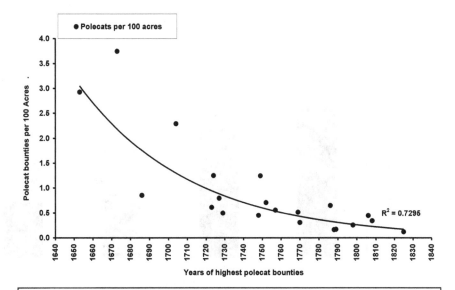

Figure 2. Declining density of polecats from the seventeenth to the nineteenth century as illustrated by plotting the highest number of polecat bounties per 100 acres within decades from 1640 to 1840

The Polecat as a Lowland species

Based on anecdotal allusions in the nineteenth century literature, Howes (1980) suggested a former preference for lowland parishes and wetland habitats. Aggregating vermin bounty data into four altitude categories, confirms the polecat's association with lowland parishes (see Figure 3).

Parliamentary Enclosure Awards and the drainage of wetlands

The parliamentary enclosure awards from the mid-eighteenth century to the mid-nineteenth century had a profound effect on the pattern of the Yorkshire landscape and its ecology, bringing in excess of 1 million acres of common land with its mosaics of uncultivated grassland, scrub, woodland and wetland under intensive agricultural or game and sporting management.

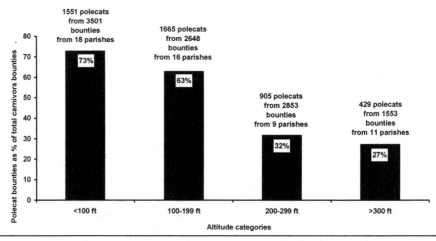

Figure 3. Relationship between altitude of parish (as determined by altitude of parish church) and Polecat as % of carnivora bounties (based on Howes 2009)

Drainage and land improvement, a frequent requirement and by-product of enclosure award schemes, flourished during this period. Drainage and first attempts to cultivate the Doncaster Carrs commenced during the mid-1700s, a period when similar schemes were being undertaken in wetland areas throughout lowland Yorkshire, examples being in the Vale of Pickering and the Hull Valley (Sheppard, 1958). These developments coincided with the disappearance as breeding species of the bittern *Botaurus stellaris* 'which deserted the [Doncaster] Carrs' about the 1750s (Hatfield, 1866) and the marsh harrier *Circus aeruginosus* 'which formerly bred on the wastes around Doncaster and the East Riding', but was 'compelled to retreat before the spread of agriculture ...' (Nelson, 1907). With polecats showing a lowland, often waterside, preference, preying on a range of aquatic and amphibious vertebrates, they were no doubt hard hit by these revolutionary changes. Hatfield (1866), discussing the decline of the polecat on the Doncaster Carrs, claimed that 'the cultivation of land has been a most formidable enemy in its destruction'.

In the parish of Wadworth, which encroaches on to the Doncaster Carrs, there were two enclosure awards, one of 1,962 acres in 1767, the other of 4,000 acres in 1771. Figure 4a shows that both of these events coincided with marked increases in polecat bounty payments within the parish suggesting that during these episodes of agricultural disturbance and the denudation of the local fens and willow copses, the local polecats became vulnerable to capture. Furthermore, polecat bounty numbers slumped during the following three decades for which vermin records are available. Similarly, in the lowland parish of Cottingham, East Yorkshire, a 3,000-acre enclosure award was enacted in 1771 and one of 1,532 acres in 1793. Figure 4b shows a similar pattern to that caused by the Wadworth inclosures.

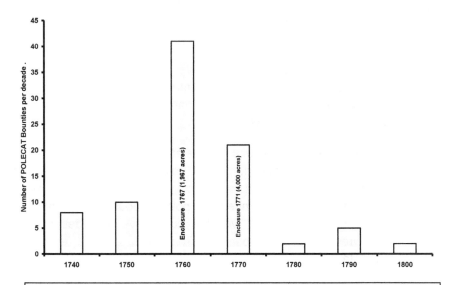

Figure 4a. Polecat bounties paid per decade in the parish of Wadworth, showing an increase in persecution during the Enclosure Awards of 1767 and 1771

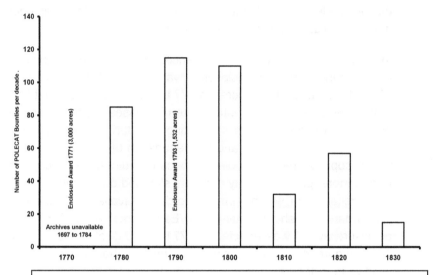

Figure 4b. Polecat bounties paid per decade in the parish of Cottingham, showing a decline following the Enclosure Awards of 1771 and 1793

Thus, it is possible that large scale and widespread landscape disturbance, during the implementation of the parliamentary enclosure awards, may have instigated unsustainable culling of polecats across the Yorkshire region.

A negative relationship (with a correlation coefficient of over 0.82) between the population density of polecats and the progressive spread of enclosure landscapes is indicated in Figure 5 which compares the mean numbers of polecat bounty payments per parish (in Howes, 2009) with the cumulative acreages of new enclosures in Yorkshire parishes from 1760 to 1849 (estimated from data in English 1985).

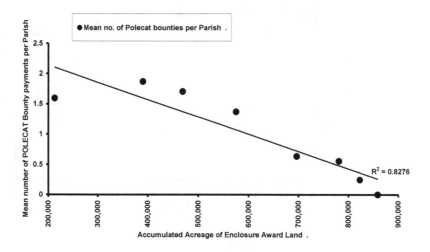

Figure 5. Comparison between the mean numbers of Polecat bounty payments per parish with the cumulative acreages of new enclosures in Yorkshire parishes from 1760 to 1849 (estimated from data in English 1985)

Intra-guild competition between Polecats and Foxes:

With the reputation of polecats as predators of game birds, particularly of young pheasants, in some quarters foxes were encouraged on the pretext that they were thought to kill polecats (Langrigg, 1977). An analysis of vermin bounty records provides evidence of competition between polecats and foxes (Howes, 2009). Figure 6 indicates that when the fox component of the carnivore bounties rose above 12%, (as at Wadworth), the proportion of polecats began to decline.

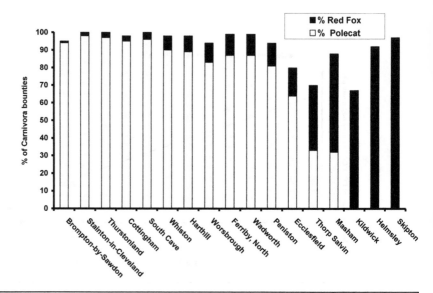

Figure 6. Seventeen Yorkshire Parishes where bounties were paid for both Polecat and Fox arranged in increasing % frequency of Fox bounties

Land acquired by major estates and landowners during the period of the parliamentary enclosures was sometimes used to develop fox coverts with the purpose of providing managed earths for rearing foxes. Since many hunt territories and their coverts were in lowland regions, the eighteen and nineteenth centuries saw the fox expand its distribution from upland Pennine regions into lowland areas (see Figure 7) thus competing with polecats for food and denning sites.

Fox Coverts

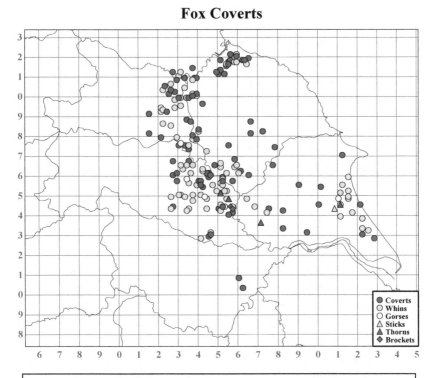

Figure 7. Distribution of eighteen and nineteenth century Fox Coverts, Whins, Gorses, Sticks, Thorns and Brockets, based on early Ordnance Survey and fox hunting literature (from Howes, 2009)

Evidence of a National recovery:

Tapper (1992) estimated that prior to the First World War there had been between 4 and 8 gamekeepers per 100 km² across East Yorkshire. With the effects of the two World Wars and industrialisation of post-war farming, gamekeeping has been substantially marginalized. Estimating that in 1981, North Yorkshire only supported between 2 to 4 keepers per 100 km² and the south, west and east of Yorkshire had less than 1 per 100 km². Significantly, a small batch of Yorkshire polecat records was claimed soon after the Second World War though any revival was short-lived (Howes, 1980). However, at the same time, Welsh populations increased greatly and proceeded to spread to adjacent English counties (Walton, 1977).

The Boys are Back in Town!

The series of British Mammal atlases (Walton, 1964 to Arnold, 1993) monitored the early stages of the spread of polecats from their north Welsh post-nineteenth century *refugium* to the adjacent English counties. The highly publicised surveys of polecat distribution in Britain 1993-1997 (Birks & Kitchener, 1999) and 2004-2006 (Birks 2008), organised by the Vincent Wildlife Trust in association with the Mammal Society, provide the first evidence of verifiable polecats in and adjacent to the extreme western and south-western fringes of Watsonian Yorkshire since the nineteenth century.

(The Cumbrian Connection) Of the post-1989 polecat records gathered by Birks & Kitchener (1999), one was from the Garsdale area, within north-west Yorkshire (VC65). From the records of true polecats gathered during the 2004-2006 survey (Birks 2008), one was from the Ingleton area within mid-west Yorkshire (VC64). Birks & Kitchener (1999) also recorded true polecats from the following 10 km squares adjacent to Watsonan Yorkshire - NY/72, NY/60, NY/70 and SD/67. The 2004-2006 survey (Birks, 2008) also recorded true polecats from the adjacent 10 km squares NY/71, SD/58, SD/57 and SD/54. All these occurrences are deemed to be part of a population derived from reintroductions into the Cumbrian region since the 1970s.

(The Derbyshire Connection) Emanating from the Welsh population, the first post-nineteenth century Derbyshire record was a road casualty at Church Broughton (SK/2033) in June 1993 (Moyes, 1994) and many more records have followed, indeed the 2004-2006 survey (Birks 2008) recorded true Polecats of the Welsh phenotype in the following 10 km squares adjacent to South Yorkshire: SK/09, SK/18 and SK/27. Dark coloured (polecat-like) animals recorded in the Sorby Natural History Society area 1970 to

1997 were mapped by Clinging & Whiteley (1997). These have also been included in Figure 8 but as polecat-ferret hybrids.

Polecat in Watsonian Yorkshire 2000-2010

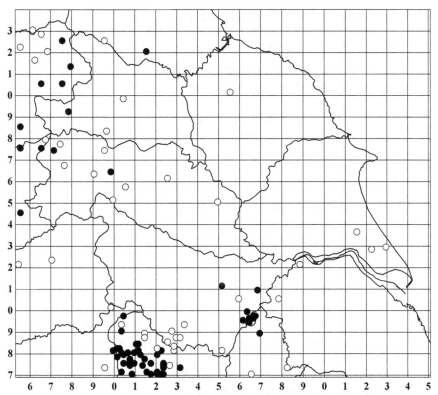

Figure 8. Distribution of Welsh phenotype Polecats (•) and unconfirmed or Ferrety Polecat records (mainly road casualties) (○)

The status of feral polecat-ferrets and wild polecats is clearly at a dynamic stage and constant monitoring is required to keep pace with this fast moving situation.

References

Arnold, H.R. (1993) *Atlas of Mammals in Britain*. Institute of Terrestrial Ecology, Abbots Ripton.

BBC TV (2009) BBC1 'Springwatch' appeal for records of Polecats.

Birks, J.D.S. (2008) *The Polecat Survey of Britain 2004-2006: report on the Polecat's distribution, status and conservation.* The Vincent Wildlife Trust, London.

Birks, J.D.S. & Kitchener, A.C. (1999) *The distribution and status of the polecat Mustela putorius in Britain in the 1990s.* Vincent Wildlife Trust, London.

Clinging, V. & Whiteley, D. (1997) Distribution maps of Sheffield area Mammals. *Sorby Record*, **33,** 2-35.

Howes, C.A. (1980) Aspects of the history and distribution of polecats and ferrets in Yorkshire and adjacent areas. *Naturalist*, **105**, 3-16.

Howes, C.A. (2009) *Changes in the status and distribution of mammals of the Order Carnivora in Yorkshire from 1600.* Unpublished PhD Thesis, University of Bradford, Bradford.

English, B.A. (1985) *Yorkshire Enclosure Awards*. Studies in Local History No. 5. University of Hull, Hull.

Hatfield, C.W. (1866) *Historical Notices of Doncaster*. Doncaster Gazette, Doncaster.

Langley, P.J.W. & Yalden, D.W. (1977) The decline of the rarer carnivores in Great Britain during the nineteenth century. *Mammal Rev.*, **7**, 95-116.

Langrigg, R. (1977) *The English Squire and his Sport*. Michael Joseph, London.

Lovegrove, R. (2007) *Silent Fields: the long decline of a nation's wildlife.* Oxford University Press, Oxford.

Moyes, N. (1994) *Derbyshire Mammal Group Newsletter*, **4** (4), 11.

Nelson, T. (1907) *The Birds of Yorkshire*. Brown, Hull.

Oxford, G., Mortimer, J., Hanson, A., Pickles, S. & Thompson, M. (2007) Preliminary mapping of terrestrial mammal distributions in North Yorkshire 1996-2006. *Naturalist*, **123**, 73-99.

Sheppard, J.A. (1958) The draining of the Hull Valley. *E. Yorks. Local Hist. Soc. Series*, **8**.

Tapper, S. (1992) *Game Heritage: an ecological review of shooting and gamekeeping records*. Game Conservancy, Fordingbridge.

Thompson, M. (2002) The Pine Marten in North-East Yorkshire? *Ryedale Natural History Society*
http://www.ryenats.org.uk/marten02.htm

Walton, K.C. (1964) The distribution of the polecat (*Putorius putorius*) in England, Wales and Scotland, 1959-62. *Proc. Zool. Soc. Lond.*, **143**, 333-336.

Walton, K.C. (1977) *Polecat and ferret*. In: Corbet, G.B. & Southern, H.N. (eds.) *The Handbook of British Mammals*. 2nd ed. Blackwell, Oxford.

BLACK-HEADED BUNTING.

The Changing Face of Breeding Birds in Yorkshire
– a brief review 2012

Keith Clarkson
RSPB

Introduction

Yorkshire has a strong history of amateur natural history recording, which makes it possible to map many of the changes that have occurred in the breeding avifauna of the county during the last 150 years. This paper aims to briefly review these changes and identify the key factors that have driven them and make recommendations for the future conservation of the County's breeding birds.

Figure 1. Common Crane - back in Yorkshire once again
© Ian D. Rotherham

Changes in the diversity of breeding birds

At the start of the twentieth century, 123 species were known to breed in Yorkshire (Nelson, 1907). In the previous one hundred years, Nelson noted the loss of Bittern, Great Bustard, Red Kite, Avocet, Stone Curlew, Ruff, Black-tailed Godwit, Wryneck and Chough as breeding birds. By the 1950s the number of reported breeding birds had increased to 134 species (Chislett, 1952) but Woodlark, Red-backed Shrike and Raven had been lost and by the 1980's Mather reported 138 breeding species (Mather, 1986). New additions to the breeding fauna included: Wigeon, Goosander, Goshawk, Common Gull, Fieldfare, Siskin and Collared Dove; whilst Spotted Crake and Corncrake had temporarily been lost as breeding species in the intervening years.

Remarkably, since Mather's excellent review, in the last ten years, the total number of species reported breeding or attempting to breed has increased to *c.*160 species with the addition of Egyptian Goose, Mandarin Duck, Little Egret, Red Kite, Spotted Crake, Corncrake, Common Crane, Avocet, Mediterranean Gull, Rose-ringed Parakeet, Cetti's, Savi's and Marsh Warblers, Golden Oriole, Raven and Common Rosefinch amongst others. However, this has been accompanied by the loss of Hen Harrier, Nightingale and Black Redstart (Thomas, 2012).

The factors driving these historical changes in Yorkshire's bird populations are inevitably complex. Many can be accounted for by wetland loss, agricultural intensification, afforestation, human persecution, and the natural fluctuations associated with species breeding at the edges of their geographic range.

Monitoring changes in the numbers of breeding birds

Superficially, the increase in the diversity of breeding birds suggests a positive picture. However the real story lies in the changes to the breeding populations of birds in the wider Yorkshire countryside that have occurred and are still doing so.

To help understand these, often more subtle changes, we have to turn to the results of the British Trust for Ornithology's (BTO) Common Bird Census (CBC) and, more recently, the BTO/JNCC/RSPB Breeding Bird Survey (BBS), which has become the main scheme for monitoring the population changes of the UK's common and widespread breeding birds during the period 1994–2011. Based upon the observations of hundreds of volunteer bird surveyors the BBS produces annual population trends, for over 100 bird species and provides an important indicator of the health of the countryside. Trends are produced for the four separate countries within the UK, and for regions, within England, thus helping to identify how trends vary spatially and, for the purpose of this paper, within Yorkshire and Humberside.

The results, which are available on the BTO website, show that in 2011, of the 49 species for which trends can be calculated in this region, the Rook has shown the greatest decline, and Oystercatcher the greatest increase. Moorhen, Woodpigeon, Coal Tit, Long-tailed Tit, Blackbird and Reed Bunting have all shown greater increases than in other English regions, and Yorkshire is the only region in which Skylark has not declined. Great Spotted Woodpecker and Whitethroat increased less than in other English regions. On the other hand, Grey Heron, Kestrel, Magpie, Rook and Pied Wagtail, all declined more than in other regions.

Factors driving change in Yorkshire's bird populations

Climate Change
Across Europe, species associated with warmer temperatures are typically showing more positive trends than those species associated with cool temperatures, an effect that is becoming apparent in Yorkshire. In 2009, almost inconceivable thirty years ago, Little Egret bred in Yorkshire for the first time. In 2008, a male Dartford Warbler held a territory on a moorland fringe of the Peak District and Hobby, Woodlark and Cetti's Warbler continue their northward expansion across the county. Whilst, prior to the severe winters of 2010 and 2011, the Stonechat underwent a spectacular expansion in its breeding range across many parts of Yorkshire, including the Sheffield area where the range increase was from 4% of the area in 1980 to 31% in 2008 (Hill & Woods in prep.).

Changing patterns of agricultural and intensification
Agricultural intensification, specifically the use of herbicides and pesticides, the shift to autumn sown cereals and subsequent loss of winter stubbles, the loss and deterioration of hedgerows and the loss of mixed farming system, upland hay meadows, permanent pasture and heterogeneity in the farmed landscape have all

contributed to a continued national decline in farmland birds (Figure 3).

Figure 2. A victim of farming change – the Corncrake
© Ian D. Rotherham

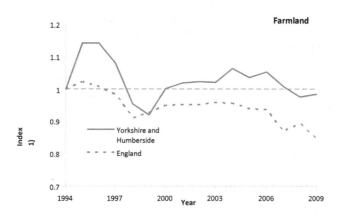

Figure 3. Breeding Bird Survey (BBS) population indices for farmland birds in England and Yorkshire and Humberside from 1994-2009 (BTO/ JNCC/ RSPB)

Here in Yorkshire, the farmland bird indicator has seen a steady decrease after showing signs of recovery from 1999 to 2004. Seven of the species indices included in this indicator are in decline including Grey Partridge, Skylark, Yellowhammer, Corn Bunting and Yellow Wagtail and eight are increasing. Of these species, Starling and Rook have shown the greatest declines (greater than 50 per cent), and Goldfinch, Wood Pigeon, Stock Dove and Jackdaw the greatest increases.

Whilst in the uplands the 75-80% loss of hay meadows on the moorland fringe has driven the virtual extinction of the Twite across much of its former range. The English breeding population has been reduced to *c*. 100 pairs of which 70 pairs breed in the Halifax area where artificial feeding schemes have been initiated to supplement the diet of breeding birds. It is evident that public funding through agri-environment schemes has failed to reverse the declines in many specialist farmland breeding birds.

Changing patterns of sea fishery management
Continuous reductions in the Yorkshire fishing fleet over the last thirty years have had a surprising impact on some seabird populations. Ironically, as the levels of fishing activity have declined across the UK so have the coastal populations of Fulmar and Herring Gull. At Flamborough Head and Bempton Cliffs, the Fulmar population has declined from over 1,200 pairs in 2000 to just over 800 pairs in 2010. Similarly, the Herring Gull has undergone a forty year decline from 1,246 pairs in 1989 to less than 600 pairs in 2009 (Clarkson, 2010). It is likely that these declines are driven by the ongoing reduction in discards from the fishing boats.

Wetland habitat loss, creation and management
In the last 400 years, the lowland landscape of much of Yorkshire has changed beyond recognition. In 1626 Vermuyden and his Dutch colleagues started to drain the 70,000 acre fenlands of Hatfield Chase whilst 4,000 acres of Potteric Carr fell to Smeaton and his engineers in 1764. Elsewhere farmers drained the Vales of Pickering, York and Mowbray, the Hull Valley and Holderness and the wider Humberhead Levels (Rotherham, 2010).

The draining of Yorkshire's great fenlands led to the loss of breeding Bittern, Marsh Harrier, Crane, Ruff, Black-tailed Godwit and Bearded Tit. Whilst on the uplands the systematic cutting of moorland grips across the blanket peat and agricultural intensification of the moorland fringe contributed to major declines in the number of breeding Teal, Snipe, Redshank, Dunlin and Black-headed Gull.

Figure 4. Bittern, lost for a century but now back and breeding © Ian D. Rotherham

However, in the last fifty years we have witnessed one of the most successful conservation stories in Yorkshire's history. The creation and management of a network of wetland reserves at Blacktoft Sands, Fairburn Ings and St Aidan's in the Aire Valley, Old Moor, Edderthorpe, Adwick and Houghton Washlands in the Dearne Valley, all managed by the RSPB, the Lower Derwent Valley and Thorne and Hatfield Moors National Nature Reserves managed by Natural England and Potteric Carr and North Cave Wetlands, managed by the Yorkshire Wildlife Trust. These have enabled the recovery and return of breeding Bittern, with at least five pairs in 2012, Marsh Harrier – a minimum of 33 pairs in 2011, Spotted Crake – six territorial males in 2011, Avocet – *c.* 50 pairs in 2011, Common Crane two pairs in 2012 and a pair of Mediterranean Gull in 2011, Cetti's Warbler at least two pairs in 2012 and three reeling Savi's Warbler at Blacktoft Sands in 2011. Furthermore, Yorkshire now supports the second highest population of Black-necked Grebes in the UK.

Loss of woodland structure and management

Despite extensive post-war planting of deciduous woodland approximately a third of woodland species including Garden Warbler, Willow Tit, Redstart and Pied and Spotted Flycatcher have undergone declines in population size and or contracted their range in the last two or three decades.

Two of the most likely factors to have influenced these declines are the lack of heterogeneity in the structure of the woodland and the loss of understorey habitat. Such changes have been brought about by the lack of woodland management and the increased browsing pressure created by escalating numbers of deer. The latter reduces the invertebrate availability and removes potential nest sites.

However, these changes are unlikely to have driven the declines in Lesser Spotted Woodpecker and Hawfinch populations. Ironically, here the cause may lie in the increasing populations of many resident woodland breeding birds (Figure 5) e.g. Great Spotted Woodpecker, Nuthatch, Chiffchaff (which has increased by 100 percent since the baseline for the BBS was established in 1994), Robin, Blue and Great Tit, and mammals, notably Grey Squirrel. The latter has in turn generated increased predation and competition for food and nest-sites.

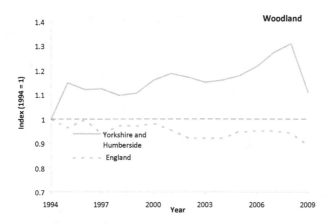

Figure 5. Breeding Bird Survey (BBS) population indices for woodland birds in England and Yorkshire and Humberside from 1994-2009 (BTO/ JNCC/ RSPB).

The extensive planting of commercial forestry across large areas of Yorkshire and the wider UK in the 20th century has also had a significant impact. The presence of Larch, various species of Pine, Spruce and Fir in the landscape has enabled the spectacular spread of Siskin and Crossbill. Whilst the management of mature plantations by open fell clearance has enabled the population of Nightjar in areas such as the North York Moors to reach nationally significant levels.

Loss of habitat and changes in migratory stop-over and wintering areas

In the late 1960s, the breeding population of Common Whitethroat and Sand Martin crashed in response to persistent drought conditions in the arid Sahel region which lies south of the Sahara, in Africa. The rains have since returned to the Sahel and breeding populations of birds are once again increasing with the notable exceptions of Turtle Dove and Yellow Wagtail which both winter in the Sahel. In the Sheffield area alone the Turtle Dove has undergone a 91% reduction in breeding range since 1980 (Hill and Woods in prep).Interestingly, some areas of Yorkshire seem to be bucking the trend for these latter two species with both the Turtle Dove population in the afforested areas of the southern North York Moors and the Yellow Wagtail population in the arable chalk-land of the Yorkshire Wolds undergoing significant increases.

However, once again many of the UK's long-distance migrants, including Cuckoo, Nightingale and both Garden and Wood Warbler and Spotted and Pied Flycatcher, are in rapid decline. It is interesting to speculate that these declines, which are evident across much of Yorkshire, may be primarily driven by changes to their wintering areas which they share in the more humid regions in West and Central Africa (Ockendon *et al.*, 2012).

Persecution and bird protection and re-introductions

Historically, many birds of prey, owls and water-birds have come into conflict with human interests over game-birds, pigeon-racing, livestock management or commercial and leisure fisheries. Whilst others, such as the seabirds at Flamborough and Bempton Cliffs, suffered at the hands of fashion, sport shooting and commercial egg collection.

Now, thanks to legislative changes and changed attitudes many species have seen dramatic recoveries not only in Yorkshire but across the UK, typified by the spectacular rise in the Common Buzzard breeding population in Yorkshire and Humberside. This showed an increase in the BBS squares between 1994 and 2009 of 1,782 percent.

Similarly, an ambitious programme to reintroduce breeding Red Kite, based on the Harewood Estate in West Yorkshire, in 1991 has been an outstanding success. In 2010, a remarkable 84 breeding pairs were located across East, West and South Yorkshire, raising 147 fledged young (Thomas, 2012).
Whilst on the east coast of Yorkshire, this protection and the lack of disturbance has enabled England's only breeding Gannet colony, at the RSPB's Bempton Cliffs reserve to increase from 22 pairs in the 1970's to over 11,000 pairs in 2012.

However, it is not all good news and many birds of prey are absent from large swathes of suitable moorland habitat. The absence of the Hen Harrier, and Goshawk, from virtually all driven grouse-moors implies that illegal persecution is driving the extinction of the Hen Harrier as a breeding bird in Yorkshire and England.

Diseases

The impact of disease on wild bird populations is not normally regarded as a major factor influencing our changing avifauna populations. However, *Trichomonosis* is probably the most significant disease impact ever recorded on a wild bird species in the UK. Since its emergence in 2005, the national Greenfinch breeding population has declined by 35% between 2005 and 2009, and the decline in those areas with the highest disease intensity has been even more pronounced. And, because the disease is still circulating, the true figure may be nearer one half or higher.

Non-native species

Several new additions to the Yorkshire avifauna are non-native species which have their origins as birds that have escaped or been deliberately introduced to the wild from captivity and have since established sustainable breeding populations. These include long established species such as the Canada Goose and species such as Greylag Goose and Ruddy Duck which became established in the 1970's and, more recently, an increasing population of Mandarin Duck and occasional feral Barnacle Goose and Egyptian Goose. It is likely that Rose-ringed Parakeets are now occasionally breeding in Yorkshire.

Figure 6. Ring-necked or Rose-ringed Parakeet by Chris Hurst (via Ian Rotherham)

Game management

Release of Common or Ring-necked Pheasants into the UK landscape has increased approximately fivefold since the early 1960s (Game and Wildlife Conservation Trust) and is now running at around 35 million birds annually. High Pheasant densities potentially have negative effects on native UK birds, although this has not been adequately studied. These include their effect on the structure of the field layer, the spread of disease and parasites, and competition for food. Infection with caecal nematodes from farm-reared Pheasants may be contributing to the decline of Grey Partridge in Britain and Yorkshire.

Other significant changes in bird populations

The above review identifies some of the key changes in the breeding avifauna of Yorkshire and highlights some of the key factors driving these changes. However, there are fundamental changes where the factors driving the change are still largely unknown. For example, research is being carried out by the BTO, RSPB and numerous academic organisations to better understand the causes of the declines in the Cuckoo, Lesser Spotted Woodpecker, Swift, Willow Warbler, Whinchat and Mistle Thrush for example.

Conclusions

By the early 2000s, the number of breeding bird species in Yorkshire is probably higher than at any time in living memory. Direct conservation management through NNRs, nature reserves and targeted conservation action has helped bring back many species from the edge but many reserves are isolated and costly to manage.

Despite the conservation successes, declining populations continue to be a feature of our wider countryside. Broad and shallow environmental payments for farmers have largely failed to halt the losses faced by many of our farmland birds and many of our woodland bird populations are also undergoing declines. Birds of prey, attempting to breed on many of our upland moors, remain the victims of illegal persecution.

To overcome these challenges there is a need to:

- Work together to build networks of reserves that can be managed as an integrated unit alongside targeted conservation projects that can deliver habitats and species management on a landscape scale both on land at sea;
- Improve agri-environment schemes particularly around options choice and management delivery. But the more fundamental questions that need to be considered are about the future of the European Common Agricultural Policy and whether public funding is used to deliver broad and shallow agri-environmental management across the farmed landscape or whether it is targeted at what become farmed reserves allowing the wider countryside to focus on food production. Whatever, choices and decisions are made, they will continue to have an impact on Yorkshire's changing farmland bird populations;
- Develop a better understanding of the changes affecting our woodland birds and incorporate the findings into the management of the woodland network;

- Deliver an alternative vision for the management of our uplands which restores and regenerates our internationally important peatlands, moorland cloughs and in-bye farmland; and
- Continue to inspire people about the extraordinary birds and wildlife that make Yorkshire so unique.

References

Chislett, R. (1952) *Yorkshire Birds*. A. Brown and Sons, London

Clarkson, K. (2010) The Flamborough Head and RSPB Bempton Cliffs SPA Seabird Colony Census 2008, *Yorkshire Bird Report,* **2008**, 167-175

Davey, C.M, Vickery, Boatman, N.D., Chamberlain, D.E., Parry, H.R., & Siriwardena, G.M. (2010) Assessing the impact of Entry Level Stewardship on lowland farmland birds in England. *Ibis*, **150**, 585-595

Gibbons, D.W, Reid J.B. & Chapman, R.A. (1993) *The New Atlas of Breeding Birds in Britain and Ireland: 1988-1991*. T & A.D. Poyser, London

Holloway, S. (1996) *The Historical Atlas of Breeding Birds in Britain and Ireland: 1875-1900*, T & A D Poyser, London

Mather, J.R. (1986) *The Birds of Yorkshire (1986)* Croom Helm

Nelson, T.H., (1907) *The Birds of Yorkshire*, A. Brown and Sons

Ockendon, N., Hewson, C.M., Johnston, A. & Atkinson, P.W. (2012) Declines in British-breeding populations of Afro-Palearctic migrant birds are linked to bioclimatic wintering zone in Africa, possibly by constraints on arrival time advancement. *Bird Study*, **59:2**, 111-125

Risely, K., Massimino, D., Johnston, A., Newson, S.E., Eaton, M.A., Musgrove, A.J., Noble, D.G., Procter, D. & Baillie, S.R., (2012) The Breeding Bird Survey 2011. *BTO Research Report*, **624**, British Trust for Ornithology, Thetford

Rotherham, I.D. (2010) *Yorkshire's Forgotten Fenland*. Wharncliffe Books, Barnsley

Sharrock, J.T.R. (1976) *The Atlas of Breeding Birds in Britain and Ireland.* T & A D Poyser, London

Thomas, C.C. (2012) *Yorkshire Bird Report 2010.* YNU.

**Figure 7. The cliffs and Flamborough in the early 1900s
(© Ian Rotherham)**

Sustainability or Bust:
The Fall and Rise of The Don's Fish Population

Chris Firth

Don Catchment Rivers Trust, Formerly Environment Agency

The River Don provided the source of prosperity to South Yorkshire for hundreds of years, but the river paid a high price by having its physical environment seriously damaged, its waters grossly polluted and its wildlife population all but eliminated. Whilst some grew rich on this prosperity, the majority of the inhabitants of the valley suffered the consequences of living in a degraded environment, the loss of a major recreational resource and, for many the pollution of their main source of drinking water. These conditions, which reached a peak at the beginning of the twentieth century, persisted for more than 150 years and it was not until the late 1980s that clear signs of recovery began to emerge.

Figure 1. Salmon leaping

A quarter of a century later salmon are once more frequenting the waters of the River (Figure 1). This most iconic of fish species that 250 years ago was so abundant in the River Don has at last returned. Presently the species is a regular visitor rather than an established self- sustaining population but the very fact that these fish are present in the river is testimony to the amazing improvements that have been achieved in water quality during the last 25 years. However, if we delve back into the history of salmon on the Don it is clear that it was not water quality that originally destroyed their populations. Some 700 years before the urbanisation and development driven by the industrial revolution rendered the waters of the Don polluted and unable to sustain fish, early industry in the form of weirs to power water mills was beginning to restrict the upstream movement of migratory fish and prevent them reaching their natural spawning grounds.

By the middle of the eighteenth century, this development was so advanced that is recorded that there were 161 weirs on the Don and its tributaries upstream of the centre of Sheffield (Figure 2). Faced with such formidable obstacles it was not long before populations of salmon and other migratory species began to decline and ultimately disappear from the system. As previously mentioned, water quality has improved to the extent that salmon, a species requiring very clean water conditions are now able to exist in the river. That is not to say that all of the issues relating to water quality have been overcome, far from it, but the very presence of salmon is a strong indication that the main sources of pollution have been, or are being, brought under control.

Figure 2. Typical Weir

Figure 3. Crimpsall

The salmon which are presently entering the Don system do not represent a self-sustaining population. To date they have only managed to ascend as far as the weir at Sprotborough. Their presence here was only made possible by the construction of huge a fish pass at Doncaster (Figure 3).

This structure that replaced a sluice, which had previously replaced a large weir, provided free passage at this point on the river for the first time in more than 800 years. Novel in its design this fish pass was built by the Environment Agency in the year 2000. The structure, which is 130m long, takes out a head difference of 3.5 metres. The pass is constructed of large lumps of limestone, which help to slow the flow by creating friction. Each lump of stone acts as a barrier to flow. Rather like standing behind a wall in a strong wind, fish simply move from one refuge to the next until they ascend the structure. The pass cost almost £1.5 million and this helps to demonstrate the level of investment that will be needed to address fish passage on the remaining 44 weirs which still exist upstream of Sprotborough. It is estimated that the average cost of fitting fish passes on these structures will be around £500K. This may present a bleak prospect but there are opportunities too. Four of the five structures immediately upstream of Sprotborough have been identified as suitable for the development of hydro power and proposals have been put forward for this development, which would include the installation of fish passage facilities. The fifth one at Ickles, Rotherham is the subject of a planning proposal which also includes a fish pass. When these proposals come to fruition fish will have the opportunity to ascend the river to the outskirts of Sheffield. Here too work is underway to provide them passage (Figure 4).

Figure 4. Hadfields weir, Meadowhall

The Don Catchment Rivers Trust has been awarded funding from DEFRA to build a pass on Hadfields Weir adjacent to the Meadowhall complex. The Trust, are working in collaboration with the Environment Agency and the owners of the Meadowhall site and this scheme is expected to be completed by September 2012. Upstream of here are another eight weirs before we reach the confluence of the River Loxley, the first tributary believed to be capable of providing suitable conditions for salmon to reproduce. The Trust is awaiting confirmation of funding to undertake outline designs for these structures.

Under existing legislation the Environment Agency can insist that fish passage facilities are installed on a weir where it has to be repaired or rebuilt over more than 50% of its length. However, this directive can only be applied where migratory salmonids are present. The legislation is recognised as out-dated and inadequate and a new bill is expected to be enacted within the next 3 to 4 years. This will make it a condition that fish passes are constructed on all weirs that prevent fish movement. This new legislation will assist the Environment Agency in achieving its targets for meeting the requirements of the Water Framework Directive. The target date for addressing all obstructions to fish passage is 2021, a formidable challenge, when you consider that there are 1,500 obstructions on rivers in the North East Region alone.

So far, I have focussed almost solely on salmon but it is not just this species, which is affected by barriers to movement. Over the last 20 years populations of most of the 27 species which were recorded as indigenous to the River Don system have been re-introduced or have naturally re-populated. Take a walk along the river and it will not be long before you come upon an angler enjoying his sport. This would suggest that the populations of these species are stable and fully self-sustaining. Nevertheless, the reality is not so rosy. During extreme flood conditions, it is perfectly normal for large numbers of coarse fish, such as roach, perch, *etc.* to be swept downstream. This particularly applies to juveniles. In a natural river system, many of the fish eventually find refuge, particularly in the more benign conditions of the lower river, where a meandering course and over topping onto flood plains helps to dissipate the high velocities. As the floods abate, the fish begin to move back steadily upstream re-populating the areas they left. This sadly is not the case where the river is affected by weirs. These structures prevent any return and leave populations, in certain sections, severely depleted, and often taking several years for the populations to rebuild. In the case of the River Don, the problems besetting dislodged fish are exacerbated by channel engineering works that were carried out throughout the reaches of the middle and lower river. The most recent and extreme example was the canalisation of the river between Doncaster and Goole (Figure 5).

Figure 5. Canalised river at Barmby-Dun

This work, which took place between 1932 and 1951, resulted in the channel being shortened by more than 2 kilometres, almost 10% of its length. Those benign conditions which are normally associated with the lower sections of rivers were completely lost and replaced by an almost straight trapezoidal channel which provides little or no refuge and flow conditions which are often untenable to juvenile fish. It is interesting to note that Laman Blanchard in his publication, 'A Tour of the Don' dated 1836 described this part of the Don as wide, shallow and meandering, with reeds as far as the eye can see. This is a far cry from what exists today.

A number of schemes to address the effects of channel engineering have been carried out on the Don and its tributaries over the last two decades (Figures 6 and 7).

Figure 6. Canalised section River Dearne

Figure 7. Re-engineered channel, River Dearne

This section of the river was re-engineered in the early 1970s to address the effects of subsidence. The river, as well as having all its bends removed was also widened by over one third. The result was a sluggish, silt-ridden watercourse with little ecological potential. The scheme to address these problems focussed on narrowing the channel and re-establishing the bends with the objective of creating an environment where the more focussed flows would clear away the silt and create a substrate of gravels where species such as barbel, chub and dace, species which need clean gravels in which to lay their eggs, were able to reproduce. The reproduction of these species from this section of the Dearne now helps to support populations, both in the Dearne itself, and the parent River Don which it joins some 2 kilometres downstream.

On the Lower Don, some of the oxbows which were left following the re-engineering of the channel still exist and in one case a scheme has been carried out to re-connect this back to the river (Figure 8).

Figure 8. Oxbow section of old River Don

During extreme floods, fish are able to escape into the oxbow and seek refuge until conditions revert to normal. As well as providing a refuge for fish, the oxbow and the ponds and wetted areas created as part of the scheme now act as an important breeding and nursery area for fish and the site also caters for migrating waders and wildfowl. Sadly, the oxbow is not permanently connected to the river. The river only flows in on very large tides or during flood conditions. This is due to the scouring effects of the high velocities, which have eroded the bed of the new channel down to almost two metres below those that existed before the re-engineering.

Figure 9. Yellow Eel

One of the most threatened species on the Don is the Yellow or Common Eel (Figure 9). This species, once so prolific in the system, is now recognised as endangered on a European scale and new regulations have recently been introduced by the Environment Agency to protect it from possible extinction. What a change this is from when, in 1796, the Vicar of Thorne reported that elvers (juvenile eels) were annually, so abundant as they made their upstream migration, that on occasions they made operating water mills impossible. This may have been a slight exaggeration, but it does help to demonstrate the extent of population abundance at that time.

The demise of eel populations on the Don was not entirely caused, as may be assumed, by deteriorating water quality. In making their way upstream, following their mammoth journey from the Sargasso Sea, juvenile eels (Figure 10) were faced with the same obstacles facing other species. Weirs often created major barriers to movement, only allowing ascent when the rivers came into flood. As mentioned earlier, more than 40 of these barriers still exist on the Don itself and almost treble that number, remain on its tributaries. To address this issue, the Don Catchment Rivers Trust has been very active and to date has undertaken five projects to promote sustainable populations. Eel passes have been installed on two weirs on the River Rother and two specially designed fish friendly flap valves have been installed on outfalls from large open water bodies which provide ideal habitat for this species.

To stimulate the recovery, the Don Catchment Rivers Trust has also released more than 50,000 elvers into the wetland nature reserve at Old Moor on the River Dearne. It takes up to 15 years for eels to reach sexual maturity; and it is therefore unlikely that any of these fish will begin their journey to the Sargasso Sea until, at least, 2025.

Figure 10. Elvers,

Sadly, we are unlikely to see any substantial improvement in the populations of eels in the Don catchment for many, many years. This is not good news for the re-establishment of populations of Otter and Bittern, which rely on this fish species as part of their staple diet.

Looking forward, the prospects for fish populations on the Don have become much brighter of late. The urgency to deliver fish passes is being driven by the fact that many reaches of the river are failing to reach good ecological quality, or potential, due to the presence of weirs. It is therefore a high priority for the Environment Agency, and partners, such as the Rivers Trust, to address this issue. The challenge will be significant but the Rivers Trust has committed itself to having salmon swimming through the centre of Sheffield and entering suitable spawning areas by the year 2020 (Figure 11).

Figure 11. Salmon

It is undeniable that massive improvements have occurred on the River Don system in the last 30 years. However, there remains much to do. Continued investment in the river will be vital if we are to achieve true sustainability of fish populations. Even when we achieve this glorious vision, we need to take account of the fact that the river will continue to be heavily urbanised and run through many heavily industrialised areas. The threat of serious acute pollution incidents will always be there and vigilance must be applied, particularly when considering the potential impacts of future developments. It is a lesson that we should not forget, that the insidious destruction, which reduced the Don to become one of Europe's most polluted and physically degraded river systems was justified on the basis of social and economic benefit. This is a salutary lesson, in these times of austerity, when the emphasis is so heavily weighted towards promoting industrial and urban development.

Reference

Firth, C. (1997) *900 Years of the Don Fishery: Domesday to the Dawn of the New Millennium.* Environment Agency, Leeds.

Roadside Assistance: management and conservation of North Yorkshire's wayside flowers

Margaret Atherden
PLACE

Introduction

Margaret Atherden and Nan Sykes have carried out botanical studies of road verges in various parts of North Yorkshire, starting with a full survey of the verges of the North York Moors National Park in 1985. All verges were visited three times during the year and colour-coded according to the diversity and richness of their flora (Box 1). The top two categories of verge ('red' and 'amber') were studied in detail, with full species lists for each of the 65 red and 106 amber verges. The same methodology was used for the verges of the Howardian Hills and Vale of Pickering in 2003-4, where 17 red and 31 amber verges were recorded. Verges in Hambleton District were surveyed in 2002, with the help of volunteers from the C.M. Rob Natural History Society. A slightly different methodology was used in this case, with a list of indicator species being used to identify the top 31 verges. In 2009, a brief survey was made of the verges on the northern part of the Yorkshire Wolds, and in 2010 a similarly brief survey was made of the Yorkshire Dales' verges. A full survey of the verges of the Nidderdale AONB was carried out in 2012 and key sites were identified. Casual observations have been made elsewhere in the county, e.g. in Selby District. As a result of these studies, a good overview has now been acquired of the botanical status of North Yorkshire's road verges, which forms the background to this paper (Atherden & Sykes, 2012).

The history and management of North Yorkshire's road verges

Verges developed over the centuries in a variety of ways. Mabey (1974) traces their probable origins to the areas bounding prehistoric trackways and the more formalised embankments ('aggers') flanking Roman roads. Some of these survive today as green lanes, such as the one crossing the Pennines from Bainbridge to Oughtershaw (Figure 1). Other roads developed later from the wide drove roads along which cattle were driven to market, such as the Hambleton drove road on the North York Moors. Parliamentary Enclosure roads were a standard width, giving scope for the verges to become formalised in post-Enclosure times, when the road surfaces were converted to tarmac and the remaining areas left as rough vegetation (Figure 2). However, in the past many such verges were used for hay-cropping or informal grazing, still forming a minor but important part of the agricultural landscape. They also serve a variety of other functions, including the provision of safe passage for horses and pedestrians, routes for pipelines and other services and storage of salt and other materials.

Figure 1. Roman road from Bainbridge to Oughtershaw

Figure 2. A typical Enclosure road on the Yorkshire Wolds

BOX 1

Colour-coding of road verges

Red   Verges of very high species richness and diversity, including several regional rarities

Amber   Verges of high species richness and diversity, including a few rarities

Yellow   Verges with above average richness and diversity but not including any rarities

Green   Average verges, dominated by common species and lacking richness and diversity – the commonest category in all areas

Brown   Verges with damaged vegetation, e.g. badly trampled, or intensively managed verges in villages

Mauve   Moorland verges, where heavy grazing pressure prevents plants from reaching their normal potential

Verges comprise a suite of linear habitats, including up to five zones (Figure 3). Close to the edge of the tarmac is the 'splash' zone, where plants are regularly sprayed with mud and often salt and sometimes driven over. Plants growing here need to be adapted to this stressful regime and are typically fast-growing species with a basal rosette of leaves or a prostrate habit, e.g. greater plantain, knotgrass. Next there comes the short grass zone, which is mown regularly, followed where the verge is wide enough by the less frequently mown long grass zone. Many of the typical verge plants occur in these two zones, including most of the grasses and herbs. Many verges have a drainage ditch towards the back, which acts as a linear aquatic habitat, providing opportunities for wetland plants and animals. Some verges are bounded by a hedge bank, forming a sort of linear coppice and a habitat for woodland species.

Figure 3. Road verge in Vale of York, showing splash zone, grassy zones, drainage ditch and hedgebank with mature trees

Approximately half the plant species of North Yorkshire occur on road verges, so roadside habitats form an important element in the botanical landscape, their distributions reflecting the varying geology and soils of the county. Carboniferous Limestone on the Pennines, Jurassic limestone on the Howardian Hills and southern part of the North York Moors, and Chalk on the Wolds all support lime-loving plants, e.g. rock-rose and clustered bellflower, whilst Millstone Grit areas of the Pennines and sandstones and shales on the North York Moors are characterised by moorland plants, e.g. heathers. The heavier soils overlying glacial drift in the vales of York, Mowbray and Pickering favour plants of neutral, damper soils, including in some places wetland species, e.g. common reed.

Plants growing on verges employ various survival strategies in order to compete (Grime, Hodgson & Hunt, 1988). 'Competitors' are the aggressive colonisers that tend to dominate the short and long grass zones of verges on which they occur and prevent other species from establishing (Figure 4). Examples include hogweed and nettle. 'Stress tolerators' are slower to colonise but can survive for long periods by their ability to weather adverse conditions. They include many woodland herbs and rarities, e.g. orchids, and are found on hedge banks and in long grass zones. 'Ruderals' are adapted to disturbed habitats, particularly the splash and short grass zones, by their ability to grow and reproduce fast, e.g. dandelions and many arable weeds (Figure 5). Some of our commonest verge plants employ several different strategies, including yarrow, white clover and many grasses, e.g. cock's-foot and Yorkshire fog. Management techniques are also very important, particularly the cutting regime, as regular mowing favours grasses over most other plants. The adjacent land-use is also significant, as it determines factors such as the available seed source, the degree of shading and the amount of nutrient-rich run-off.

Figure 4. Butterbur: a competitor

Figure 5. Common poppy: a ruderal

As a result of changes in management over the years, the verge flora faces a number of problems today. Lack of regular cutting has led to many verges becoming overgrown with bracken or invaded by scrub, eliminating ruderal and other shade-intolerant species. Other verges suffer from over-cutting either by the Highways Authority cutting for road safety or by individual landowners with ride-on mowers. The timing of cutting is important for the survival of some species, e.g. common spotted orchids flowering in June or July are cut before they can set seed on some verges (Figure 6). Spray drift and run-off from farmland is a problem for some verges adjoining arable land, especially in intensive arable areas like the Vale of York. The spreading of salt in winter has resulted in the gradual spread of saltmarsh plants along many main road verges, e.g. reflexed saltmarsh grass and sea spurrey (Figure 7). Disturbance from road-works or laying of pipelines affects other sites. Deliberate planting of bulbs such as cultivated daffodils, and the escape of garden plants are altering the character of some verges, while others are suffering from the spread of invasive species, e.g. Indian balsam.

Figure 6. Verge cut at the wrong time of year, destroying orchids (surviving only in the ditch)

Figure 7. Sea spurrey (© Nan Sykes)

Conservation initiatives

Responsibility for managing verges along main roads and near dangerous junctions or bends falls to local councils, with the mowing of verges along minor roads usually contracted out to local farmers. Little attention is paid to wayside flowers in most cases. Therefore, several initiatives have been taken in recent years to raise the profile of verges and promote their conservation. The North York Moors National Park has a team of volunteers, who monitor the 'special interest verges' (the 171 originally identified in 1985 with a few later additions) and draw attention to any management requirements. The National Park Conservation Volunteers then carry out any practical work needed, e.g. scrub clearance, cutting or raking and removal of litter. In Hambleton District, volunteers from the C.M. Rob Natural History Society are monitoring the top 31 verges, as part of the district's Biodiversity Action Plan. North Yorkshire County Council (NYCC) is now managing some of these verges directly, using their countryside rangers to carry out cutting at appropriate times of year (Figure 8). However, these initiatives are piece-meal and only conserve a small proportion of road verges, so recently attempts have been made to promote good management of all road verges. NYCC staff have regular meetings with Highways Authorities and have attempted to bring about changes to the cutting policy, especially the timing of the cuts. A new contract began in 2012 but changes to the cutting regime have been limited and it remains to be seen whether county-level agreements will be implemented on the ground by sub-contractors.

Figure 8. NYCC staff discussing management with a volunteer

Another approach is to start at local level, e.g. through distribution of advice leaflets to parish councils and landowners. The NYCC website invites members of the general public to report any verges of particular interest, in the hope that they can be included in the list of special interest verges. The Yorkshire Wildlife Trust ran a very successful road verge project in collaboration with the Yorkshire Dales National Park and the Nidderdale AONB from 2008 to 2011. The project aimed to engage local communities in the management of their local verges. Over the three-year period, 250 local residents from 20 communities took part in the project, managing 86 verges, including cutting and raking and clearing scrub. A full-time officer was employed, who gave talks, led walks and produced a newsletter for local people. The funding for this project has not been renewed but it is hoped that some of the communities will continue to manage their sites from their own resources. The interest in road verges is gradually increasing; for example, North Duffield parish council are planning to manage their verges with conservation in mind.

Whilst these projects are encouraging, they are only scratching the surface. The challenge of climate change makes it imperative that plants and animals can move freely through the countryside from one site to another, through a 'living landscape', as promoted by the Wildlife Trusts' campaign. Road verges form some of the best wildlife corridors, combining grassland, woodland and wetland habitats in a network stretching throughout the country. There is now a growing awareness of the need to establish such ecological networks, as highlighted in several recent official documents (Box 2). Therefore, we need to move towards conservation of the whole road verge network, so that plants and animals can spread out from the special interest verges and colonise new areas. While botanists will always be particularly concerned with the fate of rarities, there is also a need to give greater consideration to the conservation of common species and species for which Britain is of international significance, e.g. bluebell. We should also embrace those garden escapes which are not harmful or invasive, as adding diversity to the roadside flora.

Networks of natural habitats provide a valuable resource. They can link sites of biodiversity importance and provide routes or stepping stones for the migration, dispersal and genetic exchange of species in the wider environment.
Planning Policy Statement 9: Biodiversity and Geological Conservation, 2005.

Establishing a coherent and resilient ecological network to help conserve the biodiversity that we still have will enhance our options and improve our chances of achieving a prosperous and healthy future for ourselves and our children.
'Making Space for Nature: A review of England's Wildlife Sites and Ecological Network', the Lawton Report, 2010.

We will move from net biodiversity loss to net gain, by supporting healthy, well-functioning ecosystems and coherent ecological networks.
'The Natural Choice: securing the value of nature.' Government white paper, 2011.

Conclusion

There is an increasing appreciation of the role that access to wildlife plays in human health and welfare, and of the need to reconnect people with nature. Unfortunately, over the past few years, health and safety concerns have driven many people away from roadsides and discouraged them from pursuing traditional uses of verge habitats. The best way to ensure the future survival of these roadside habitats is to use them. We should encourage people to make greater use of roadside habitats, e.g. for the informal grazing of animals (Figure 9), collecting wild fruits and nuts, walking, picnicking (Figure 10) and other types of recreation.

Road verges have suffered a major decline in their botanical interest over the past few decades. However, there is now an opportunity to reinstate them as a valued part of the landscape by engaging the general public in conservation of these accessible and fascinating parts of our natural heritage.

> *We have come through a time of significant wildlife declines but now have the opportunity to turn the tide and embrace a new, visionary restorative phase of nature conservation to create a resilient and more coherent ecological network. We are at a pivotal point.*
> **The Lawton Report, 2010.**

Figure 9. Gypsy ponies grazing a verge

Figure 10. Informal picnic on a verge

References

Atherden, M.A. & Sykes, N.M. (2012) *Wild Flowers on the Edge: The Story of North Yorkshire's Road Verges.* PLACE, York.

Grime, J.P., Hodgson, J.G., & Hunt, R. (1988) *Comparative Plant Ecology.* Unwin Hyman, London.

Lawton, Sir J. (2010) *'Making Space for Nature': a review of England's Wildlife Sites and Ecological Network.* Department for Environment Food & Rural Affairs, London.

Mabey, R. (1974) *The Roadside Wildlife Book.* David and Charles, Newton Abbott.

Red deer stag roaring by Paul Biggs on moors west of Sheffield

The Magic and Mysteries of Ecclesall Woods

Ian D. Rotherham
Sheffield Hallam University

Introduction

Ecclesall Woods is the Sheffield area's premiere ancient woodland site, and is a magical place. Locked into a major conurbation, with an area of 100 hectares it is still sufficiently large to get lost. Yet remarkably, its history and lineage have only recently been recognised. Furthermore, whilst it is now a Local Nature Reserve, and was designated as a 'Site of Scientific Interest' in the *Sheffield Nature Conservation Strategy* (1991), it has struggled to attract the support necessary for its conservation. Indeed, when South Yorkshire Forest was originally established, the Woods were deliberately excluded and the boundary drawn to the east, because the head of the Sheffield City Council Countryside Management Service considered the area 'too posh'. My argument as Principal City Ecologist, which was unsuccessful at the time, was that as the best woodland in the region it could be a showcase for woodland management and conservation. However, the argument was lost and it took another five years or so of lobbying, of fund-raising independently in order to begin vital surveys and to develop an outline interim management plan. We also held a public meeting and established the *'Friends of Ecclesall Woods'*, a vital group for the care and conservation of the site, and still thriving today. Eventually, and after several years during which the site was disadvantaged and under threat, the South Yorkshire Forest boundary was extended to include Ecclesall Woods. (The threat was because being within *South Yorkshire Forest* at that time meant access to essential funds, otherwise unavailable, for survey, and for planning and implementation).

Figure 1. Red Campion: typical woodland wild flower.
© Ian D. Rotherham

Another key landmark for the recognition of the Woods was the Landscape Conservation Forum conference on ancient woods and their archaeology and ecology in 1992. This national conference used the Woods as its case study field site and this meant that for the first time, collaborative surveys of ecology and archaeology were undertaken. These surveys were reported and the findings discussed on site. What emerged was a much-improved understanding of what was or was not known. Essentially, in terms of the archaeology of the Woods, the archaeologists generally recognised archaeology '*in*' the woods, but not '*of*' the woods. Ecologists generally did not 'see' any of the features of significance and nor did they or the foresters recognise any of the genuinely veteran trees. This set the scene for ten years of more or less intensive research with studies still on-going today. Mel Jones investigated the archives whilst Paul Ardron, I, and various helpers and postgraduates worked on field surveys of ecology and archaeology. Local naturalists and others were encouraged to survey the Woods for different taxa of plants and animals and write these up (*Peak District Journal of Natural History and Archaeology*

Special Publication, 1997; *Sorby Record*, 1992). The main archaeological surveys were completed following both private sponsorship and a Heritage Lottery Fund award (Rotherham & Ardron, 2001).

Gradually a more complete picture of this remarkable landscape was emerging. One of the original issues was that the Woods were clearly 'ancient' but botanically rather poor. Mel Jones's archival work confirmed this antiquity, as did the earlier research by Clive Hart for the 1992 conference (Hart, 1993). However, the site lacked obviously old trees and over much of the area had a depauperate ground flora. The answers lay in the history of management as coppice wood for charcoal and whitecoal manufacture over several centuries. Old, standard trees had been felled and the imposed management was coppice-with-standards, which gave underwood coppice of Oak and Hazel. There was a canopy of mainly Oak but since the trees were harvested these were only up to around 120 years old. Investigation showed the ground flora to be poor over large areas of the site and the soils to have been replaced by a layer of charcoal dust over a 'B' or 'C' horizon. Soil and vegetation had been cut, removed and, as turf, used to cover the charcoal clamps and so had been burnt (Rotherham & Doram, 1992). In other areas, especially on gentle slopes, the Woods were affected by early field systems, probably Romano-British, and the topsoils had washed off. Finally, during the 1800s and 1900s, the whole area was subjected to massive aerial pollution and deposition of soot, grit and grime (fallout of around 3.35 tons of grit and grime deposited per square mile per week in the 1920s). This caused major acidification of the soils and a decline in key woodland plants.

Figure 2. J. Bright's map of Ecclesall Woods by J. Gelley in 1725 and showing the 'laund' of the former deer park in the bottom corner.

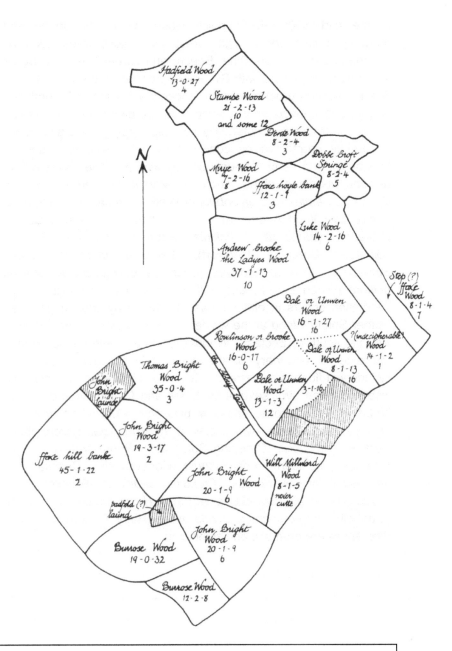

Figure 3. Map of the Eccesall Woods in the mid-1600s from Jones 1997 and showing the named 'woods'.

In the mid-1800s, the coppice woods were abandoned and gradually converted to high forest with exotic trees such as European Larch, Scots Pine, Beech, and Sweet Chestnut. Some areas were re-planted with Sycamore probably in the early 1900s. The impacts on ground flora are especially striking with combined or individual impacts on woodland soils and plants, of charcoal and whitecoal production, potentially very significant. Woodland zones apparently unaffected by coaling have well developed soil 'A' horizons with a neutral or only slightly acid pH. They have typical ancient woodland plants such as *Mercurialis perennis* (Dog's Mercury), *Lamiastrum galeobdolon* (Yellow Archangel), *Anemone nemorosa* (Wood Anemone), *Allium ursinum* (Ramsons), *Galium odoratum* (Woodruff), *Sanicula europea* (Sanicle), *Stellaria holostea* (Greater Stitchwort), *Veronica montana* (Wood Speedwell), *Circaea lutetiana* (Enchanter's Nightshade), *Melica uniflora* (Wood Melick) and *Milium effusum* (Wood Millet). This vegetation occurs in either areas unaffected by coaling (such as Nether Spring Wood at the western end of Ladies Spring Wood, a site just south of Ecclesall Woods), or as a fringing 'halo' around the external boundary of the wood. Other species-rich areas include wet flushes and streamsides. Areas influenced by intensive 'coaling' (often over several centuries and for industrial coppice), had thin 'A' horizons, and low pHs ($c.3.5$-4.5) often with raw charcoal dust directly over a clay 'B' horizon. Their typical plants were *Holcus mollis* (Creeping Soft-grass), *Rubus fruticosus* agg. (Bramble), *Lonicera periclymenum* (Honeysuckle), *Deschampsia flexuosa* (Wavy Hair-grass), *Pteridium aquilinum* (Bracken), with *Dryopteris dilatata* (Broad Buckler Fern), *Hyacinthoides non-scripta* (Bluebell), and sometimes *Luzula pilosa* (Hairy Woodrush). These differences are dramatic and significant.

Figure 4. Wild Garlic: typical wildflower of damp, shady woodland. © Ian D. Rotherham

A question of lineage and continuity: park and wood

Having established beyond doubt that Ecclesall Woods was 'ancient' woodland, there remained questions concerning its lineage and its biodiversity. We could explain the patchy ground flora and the loss of key species in relation to charcoal burning and turf stripping. However, whilst this was regarded as the region's best ancient wood, surveys of invertebrate indicators of ancient woods in the 1980s, showed Ecclesall to be surprisingly far down on the list. Ecclesall Woods lacks key species of invertebrates that its assumed antiquity would suggest that it should have. Compared with other known ancient woodland hotspots for rare saproxylic beetles and hoverflies, Ecclesall performed very badly. This raised questions about what exactly had happened and, whilst ancient, was the site indicative of continuous woodland cover. Ultimately, the meticulous site surveys by Paul Ardron combined with the archival research of Mel Jones provided answers. Following these in-depth studies of field archaeology and archival evidence, the situation made eminent sense. For long periods what is now

Ecclesall Woods was open farmland with small areas of very wet Alder carr and riverside woodland. This was the case throughout a long period from Late Neolithic, and through the Bronze Age, Iron Age, and Romano-British periods even until the late Saxon. Following the Norman Conquest, the lands changed hands and the site has its origins as a medieval hunting park. In 1317 AD, the Norman overlord, Robert de Ecclesall was granted a licence to impark, and this is reflected in modern place names such as Parkhead, Warren Wood, Park Field, and Old Park (Hart, 1993). As noted by Hart (1993), there is further evidence of the use of the Woods for hunting from a set of depositions taken on October 2nd 1587. These were from George Sixth Earl of Shrewsbury. He stated that he, his father and his grandfather:

> '.......*used sett and placed Crosbowes for to Kyll the Deare in Ecclesall Afforesaied and to hunte at all tymes when it so pleased them there.*' Thomas Creswick noted that ' ....*ye said Erle George grandfather to ye said now Erle of Shrewsbury hath sett Netts & long bowes to kill deare in Ecclesall and hunted dyvers tymes there and he thinketh that ye said Erle ffrancis father to ye Erle that now is did the lyke.*' Richard Roberts confirmed that '.....*he hath sene the lord ffrancis hunting in Ecclesall byerlow and that said lords officers sett decoers there at such places as they thought   convenyent.*'
> (Hart, 1993).

In the early 1700s, there were also livestock pastured in the Woods with horses, mares, foals, cows, heifers, calves, and sterks recorded. Gelly's map of 1725 shows a 'laund' or grazing area, in the centre of the Woods and this was planted up in 1752 (Jones & Walker, 1997). In the 1587 deposition (Hart, 1993), it is also clear that wood and underwood are also being taken, and it was this use that was to dominate the former deer park for the next few centuries. It seems the hunting use was falling from fashion by the late 1500s though there are references to deer hunts certainly from the late 1400s and early 1500s. Was this the reason for the deposition? Excitingly, in the late 1990s, Paul Ardron, working with the author, located the western boundary bank of the medieval park (Rotherham & Ardron, 2001). Here we have some insight into the evolution of a specific wooded landscape, for which the medieval imparkation was probably the critical moment in it becoming woodland today. However, this 'ancient' woodland is not all it seems, and its ecology and pedology reflect its unique history. From the 1500s onwards, the Woods were individually named and being exploited for intensive manufacture of charcoal and whitecoal. By the mid-1800s, the coppice exploitation ended. Gradually the woodland was converted to high forest with exotic tree species. It was then largely abandoned as 'amenity woodland'. This site is now locked within a sea of urbanisation and separated from its past by the process of 'cultural severance' (Rotherham, 2008, 2010). However, the key issue is that for long periods of time this site was mostly un-wooded and included large areas of arable land. For much of the rest of its history it was grazed parkland. Today, culturally severed from its working past and managed as an urban amenity space, it is rapidly becoming '*parkified*' but aside from occasional deer and rabbits, there is no grazing. Importantly, the absence of the ancient dead wood invertebrates now makes eminent sense; the site lacks essential continuity.

Bluebells and ancient woods

Despite the turf stripping and the breaks in woodland use, Ecclesall Woods is still famed for its springtime carpets of Bluebells. Adrian Vickers researched aspects of this for his PhD (Rotherham & Vickers, 1999; Vickers *et al.*, 2000; Vickers & Rotherham, 2000a); and Barry Wright, supported by the Friends of Ecclesall Woods, has undertaken detailed studies (Rotherham & Wright, 2011). Whilst Bluebells are one of the most widely recognised 'indicators' of old woodland, they do colonise quickly if they can cross boundaries and get into a site. Indeed, a reasonable sized secondary wood can be effectively colonised by Bluebell in around 200 years. In Ecclesall Woods today, the Bluebells and plants like Honeysuckle are moving back into the zones that were turf stripped by the charcoal men. The Bluebell remains an iconic and emotive species, symbolic to many visitors of ancient woods and even primeval wildwoods, whereas in reality it is recolonizing after the abandonment of traditional management. The working medieval wood was also probably more species rich until the turf was stripped, and the Bluebells dominate and exclude other species under the shady canopy of the high forest wood; all is not what it seems.

Figure 5. Bluebell – the most evocative woodland flower. © Ian D. Rotherham

Along with the Bluebell enigma, there is the issue of the trees. The biggest trees in Ecclesall Woods are Beeches and Sweet Chestnuts that date from the mid-1800s, and a handful of Chestnuts that are much older. Some old Oak coppice stools remain but whilst much older, they are generally not obvious. So again, for the visiting public this is rather confusing since the big 'ancient' trees are neither ancient nor native. The present-day treescape is a mix of an industrial past and an ornamental present. There are old Sweet Chestnuts that today look as though they were formerly coppiced and this would put back their planting in the wood to at least the early 1800s i.e. before coppice management ceased in the mid-1980s. Just a few very big old oaks survive and these do seem vulnerable to vandals setting them on fire. A handful of these trees are maybe 350 years old; they are shrunken in size because the area suffered gross air pollution from the early 1800s to at least the 1960s.

For an ancient Oak-Bluebell wood, the vegetation is often rather limited and the species-rich areas very patchy. The expected carpets of woodland flowers are markedly absent from some areas. The best sites are those peripheral zones, which avoided turf stripping and still receive light. Streamside and wet areas are generally good too. Yet a whole section of the Woods is very species-poor when topographically it looks like it should be good. The reason appears to be that here, during the 1400s to the 1800s, there was an intensive metalworking industry now evidenced by the remains of mills and other features, which simply removed the woodland flora from most of the area and it has never fully recovered. The decline of the woodland flowers was no doubt exacerbated by acid rain associated with the locally-generated air pollution.

Conclusions: putting the Woods in their context

It seems that after twenty years or more of on-going research we can answer many of the questions about Ecclesall Woods. However, there remains the issue of how this remarkable, now urban landscape, fits into the wider environment. To the immediate south flows the River Sheaf and beyond that, Ladies Spring Wood and the other ancient woods of Beauchief. Like most wooded landscapes in the city of Sheffield, the species-rich, valley-bottom woodland has long since gone. This woodland loss was associated with riverside hay-meadow cultivation in medieval times, and then of transport infrastructure and other development. A tiny fragment of wooded riverbank lies isolated and dry in an ornamental park a matter of metres on the other side of the main road from Ecclesall Woods. To the east, on the side of the main road, and at the south-east corner of Ecclesall Woods, the ancient riverbank is also visible. The River Sheaf was canalised and diverted centuries ago and the banks look out over the busy Abbeydale Road.

If we climb to the high ground of the Woods, where at the summit of the Bird Sanctuary, the escarpment faces westwards, we get a different perspective. Now wooded with Oak and an understorey of Bilberry, this slope was clearly open in prehistoric times. Beneath our feet lies a great, Iron Age hilltop enclosure, perhaps a fortified site, discovered by Paul Ardron in the 1990s. Over-lying this is an extensive and intact Romano-British field system. Clear the trees from the slope and you have a clear view over the medieval deer park pale and the Dark Ages kingdom boundary to the Peak District. Until the parliamentary enclosures of the 1700s and 1800s, this would have been an almost continual landscape of 'waste', what we now recognise as a type of wood pasture. In the far distance today, we can almost see the ancient landscapes of Longshaw. This is just at the crest of the gritstone edges as the land drops westwards to the Peak District shale valleys. Recent review of LiDAR imagery of the area confirms the scale and extent of the prehistoric and later human activity in this area. (This will be reported separately).

To the west of Ecclesall Woods, we cross the medieval deer park enclosure, and the Anglo-Saxon kingdom boundary. Then, in this upland environment of moor and pasture, and of enclosed park and hunting lodge, recent research has triggered a remarkable discovery. This is a landscape of 'shadow woods' and 'ghosts', of pasture woods, and of coppices. However, whereas in the lower-lying lands medieval woods were fixed, enclosed and named, and their survivors are today's 'ancient woods', this western zone has extensive 'shadow woods' (Rotherham, 2017). The process of enclosure and naming of the components of the medieval countryside was given authority by the 1235 Act of Commons or Statute of Merton, a 'Magna Carta of the landscape'. These 'shadow woods' of the Domesday wood pasture were never enclosed and named even after the 1235 Act of Commons gave authority to do so. They even escaped the rigorous enclosure and improvement of the 1700s and 1800s. Ancient pollard trees and stubs, whilst small in stature are probably in excess of 500 years old. These trees are therefore contemporary with the Ecclesall Deer Park and across the unenclosed 'waste' would be linked seamlessly to that landscape. This discovery extends our vision of

Ecclesall Woods from the urban, enclosed, wood of modern times and back to its roots in the medieval landscape. It also provides a new interpretation of key aspects of countryside history (Rotherham, 2017).

Figure 6. Charcoal burners' hut, Sheffield, early 1900s.
© Ian D. Rotherham

References

Anon. (1987) *Sheffield Woodland Policy*. Sheffield City Council, Sheffield.

Ardron, P.A. & Rotherham, I.D. (1999) Types of charcoal hearth and the impact of charcoal and whitecoal production on woodland vegetation. *Peak District Journal of Natural History and Archaeology*, **1**, 35-47.

Beswick, P. & Rotherham, I.D. (eds) (1993) Ancient Woodlands – their archaeology and ecology - a coincidence of interest. *Landscape Archaeology and Ecology*, **1**.

Bownes, J.S., Riley, T.H., Rotherham, I.D. & Vincent, S.M. (1991) *Sheffield Nature Conservation Strategy*. Sheffield City Council, Sheffield.

Griffiths, P. & Rotherham, I.D. (1996) *Ecclesall Woods: A Preliminary Hydrological Assessment*. Sheffield Centre for Ecology and Environmental Management, Sheffield.

Hart, C.R. (1993) The Ancient Woodland of Ecclesall Woods, Sheffield. In: Proceedings of the National Conference on Ancient Woodlands: their archaeology and ecology - a coincidence of interest, Sheffield 1992. Beswick, P. & Rotherham, I.D. (eds), *Landscape Archaeology and Ecology*, **1**, 49-66.

Jones, M. (1997) *Woodland management on the Duke of Norfolk's Sheffield estate in the early eighteenth century*. In: M. Jones (ed.) *Aspects of Sheffield: Discovering Local History*, *Vol.1*. Wharncliffe Publishing Ltd, Barnsley, 48-69.

Jones, M. (2009) *Sheffield's Woodland Heritage*. 4th Edition (revised), Wildtrack Publishing, Sheffield.

Jones, M. & Walker, P. (1997) From coppice-with-standards to high forest: the management of Ecclesall Woods 1715-1901. *Peak District Journal of Natural History and Archaeology Special Publication,* **No. 1**, 11-20.

Medforth, P. & Rotherham, I.D. (1997) The Birds of Ecclesall Woods. *Peak District Journal of Natural History and Archaeology Special Publication*, **No.1**, 21-33.

Rotherham, I.D. (1996) The sustainable management of urban-fringe woodlands for amenity and conservation objectives. *Aspects of Applied Biology*, **44**, 33-38.

Rotherham, I.D. (2005) Fuel and Landscape – Exploitation, Environment, Crisis and Continuum. *Landscape Archaeology and Ecology*, **5**, 65-81.

Rotherham, I.D. (2006) *Historic Landscape Restoration: Case Studies of Site Recovery in Post-industrial South Yorkshire, England*. In: Agnoletti, M. (ed.) *The Conservation of Cultural Landscapes*. CABI International, Wallingford, Oxfordshire, 211-224.

Rotherham, I.D. (2007) The implications of perceptions and cultural knowledge loss for the management of wooded landscapes: a UK case-study. *Forest Ecology and Management*, **249**, 100-115.

Rotherham, I.D. (2006) *Working landscapes or recreational showcases – sustainable management and the implications of cultural knowledge loss*. In: Parrotta, J., Agnoletti, M. & Johann, E. (eds) *Cultural Heritage and Sustainable Forest Management: The Role of Traditional Knowledge*. Proceedings of the Conference 8-11 June 2006, Florence, Italy, Volume 1, Published by the Ministerial Conference on the Protection of Forests in Europe, Warsaw.

Rotherham, I.D. (2008) *The Importance of Cultural Severance in Landscape Ecology Research*. In: Dupont, A. & Jacobs, H. (eds) (2008) *Landscape Ecology Research Trends*. Nova Science Publishers Inc., New York, 71-87.

Rotherham, I.D. (2010) Cultural Severance and the End of Tradition. *Landscape Archaeology and Ecology*, **8**, 178-199.

Rotherham, I.D. (2011a) *A Landscape History Approach to the Assessment of Ancient Woodlands*. In: Wallace, E.B. (ed.) *Woodlands: Ecology, Management and Conservation*. Nova Science Publishers Inc., USA, 161-184.

Rotherham, I.D. (2011b) *Animals, Man & Treescapes – perceptions of the past in the present*. In: Rotherham, I.D. &

Handley, C. (eds) (2011) Animals, *Man and Treescapes: The interactions between grazing animals, people and wooded landscapes*, Wildtrack Publishing, Sheffield, 1-32.

Rotherham, I.D. (ed.) (2012a) *Trees, Man, & Grazing Animals – A European perspective on trees and grazed treescapes.* EARTHSCAN, London.

Rotherham, I.D. (2012b) *Re-interpreting wooded landscapes, shadow woods and the impacts of grazing.* In: Rotherham, I.D. (ed.) (2012a) *Trees, Man, & Grazing Animals – A European perspective on trees and grazed treescapes.* EARTHSCAN, London.

Rotherham I.D. (2017) *Shadow Woods: A Search for Lost Landscapes.* Wildtrack Publishing, Sheffield.

Rotherham, I.D. & Ardron, P.A. (eds) (2001) *Ecclesall Woods Millenium Archaeology Project.* Sheffield Hallam University, Sheffield.

Rotherham, I.D. & Ardron, P.A. (2006) The Archaeology of Woodland Landscapes: issues for managers based on the case-study of Sheffield, England and four thousand years of human impact. *Arboricultural Journal,* **29** (4), 229-243.

Rotherham, I.D. & Avison, C. (1998) *Sustainable Woodlands for people and Nature? The relevance of landscape history to a vision of forest management.* In: *Woodland in the Landscape: Past and Future Perspectives.* Atherden, M.A. & Butlin, R.A. (eds.), The proceedings of the one-day conference at the University College of Ripon and York St John, PLACE, York, 194-199.

Rotherham, I.D. & Doram, G.P. (1992) A Preliminary Study of the Vegetation of Ecclesall Woods in Relation to Former Management. *Sorby Record,* **29**, 60-70.

Rotherham, I.D. & Egan, D. (2005) *The Economics of Fuel Wood, Charcoal and Coal: An Interpretation of Coppice Management of British Woodlands.* In: Agnoletti, M., Armiero, M., In Barca, S. and Corona, G. (eds), *History and Sustainability.* European Society for Environmental History, University of Florence, Florence, Italy, 100-104

Rotherham, I.D. & Handley, C. (eds) (2011) *Animals, Man and Treescapes: The interactions between grazing animals, people and wooded landscapes.* Wildtrack Publishing, Sheffield.

Rotherham, I.D., Jones, M., Smith, L. & Handley, C. (eds) (2008) *The Woodland Heritage Manual: A Guide to Investigating Wooded Landscapes.* Wildtrack Publishing, Sheffield.

Rotherham, I.D. & Jones, M. (2000a) Seeing the Woodman in the Trees – Some preliminary thoughts on Derbyshire's ancient coppice woods. *Peak District Journal of Natural History and Archaeology,* **2**, 7-18.

Rotherham, I.D. & Jones, M. (2000b) *The Impact of Economic, Social and Political Factors on the Ecology of Small English Woodlands: a Case Study of the Ancient Woods in South Yorkshire, England.* In: *Forest History: International Studies in Socio-economic and Forest ecosystem change.* Agnoletti, M. and Anderson, S. (eds), CAB International, Wallingford, Oxford, 397-410.

Rotherham, I.D. & Vickers, A.D. (1999) *Managing Urban Woodland - a study of the response of Bluebells to coppicing and seasonal differences between years.* Sheffield Hallam University and South Yorkshire Forest Partnership, Sheffield.

Rotherham, I.D. & Wright, B. (2011) Assessing woodland history and management using vascular plant indicators. *Aspects of Applied Biology,* **108**, 105-112.

Vickers, A.D. & Rotherham, I.D. (2000) The response of Bluebell (*Hyacinthoides non-scripta*) to seasonal differences between years and woodland management. *Aspects of Applied Biology*, **58**, 1-8.

Vickers, A.D., Rotherham, I.D. & Rose, J.C. (2000) Vegetation succession and colonisation rates at the forest edge under different environmental conditions. *Aspects of Applied Biology*, **58**, 351-356.

Figure 7. A traditional charcoal burn – sadly not in Ecclesall Woods but in Germany in the early 1900s © Ian D. Rotherham

The Cornfield Flowers Project

Rona Charles
North York Moors National Park

Introduction

The Cornfield Flowers Project is spearheaded by the Carstairs Countryside Trust (CCT), in partnership with the Ryedale Folk Museum (RFM), the North Yorkshire Moors Association and the North York Moors National Park Authority (NYMNPA) and with volunteer botanists and farmers. The Project aims to conserve and re-establish some of our rarest plants of arable fields. Botanical surveys in the 1980s by Nan Sykes and others established that most of the traditional arable 'weeds' were on the brink of extinction in the North York Moors, including: Venus' looking-glass, shepherd's needle, prickly poppy, narrow-fruited corn salad, corn buttercup (Figure 1), corn marigold (Figure 2), annual knawel, large-flowered dead-nettle, red hemp-nettle and ramping fumitory. Changes in agriculture, especially the greater use of chemical weed-killers, had stripped the fields of colour and led to the virtual elimination of many once-common cornfield flowers. Similar declines were seen throughout the country in the 1990s and it was clear that, without urgent action, this group of plants would not survive long into the twenty-first century.

Figure 1. Corn buttercup (© Nan Sykes)

Figure 2. Corn marigold (© Nan Sykes)

Phase 1: launching the project

In 1998, Nan Sykes, Ian Carstairs and Rona Charles (Ecologist with the NYMNPA) met to formulate a plan to restore some of the threatened plants. The first stage was to identify target species that were known to have grown in the National Park at the beginning of the twentieth century. Ninety-two species were identified and work began to find surviving populations of some of them within the area, using volunteers to visit local arable farms and liaise with the farmers.

The catalyst for action was the acquisition of a 25-acre field at Silpho near Scarborough, purchased with funds donated to the CCT, in memory of a former NYMNPA colleague. The initial phase lasted five years. An early success was with corn buttercup, one plant of which Nan Sykes rescued from a field of sugar beet. Fortunately, the seed germinates in the autumn and is easily grown in gardens, so seeds were collected and young plants were raised successfully. However, for the project to expand, a proper nursery was needed, and this was established at the RFM. Here volunteers created dedicated beds where rare cornfield plants could be raised for planting in other sites.

The RFM embraced the project enthusiastically, setting aside one of its fields as an artificial cornfield (Figure 3). This enabled experimental work on establishing arable plants in a cereal crop, demonstrating their varying competitive abilities and gaining experience for the volunteers in appropriate management techniques. The cornfield also proved popular with visitors to the museum, who were able to walk through the crop on mown paths and enjoy the colourful scene. On the back of this success, seeds and plugs of rare arable plants were introduced to the field margins at Silpho and the field managed in a traditional manner.

Figure 3. Cornfield at Ryedale Folk Museum (© Margaret Atherden)

Phase 2: putting the project on a more formal footing

In 2005, it was decided to apply for funding to expand the project further. A formal partnership was established between the CCT, NYMNPA and RFM and funding for a part-time project officer was obtained from the Heritage Lottery Fund and the National Park's Sustainable Development Fund. The stated aims of the project were:

- To safeguard the rare plants of arable fields in and close to the North York Moors by collecting seeds, growing the plants on and returning them to farmland;

- To raise awareness amongst the general public of the plight of arable flowers;
- To encourage farmers to use Stewardship schemes to help arable plants on their land.

A local farmer and keen conservationist, Chris Wilson, was appointed to the part time (0.5fte) post of project officer. By 2009, contact had been made with many farmers and 31 new sites had been established. Most were enthusiastic once they realised that reinstating this lost element of farming posed no risk to their crops. The original plant of corn buttercup that had been rescued by Nan Sykes eventually produced so many seeds that 2000 were lodged with the Millennium Seed Bank, a global initiative spearheaded by Kew Gardens. Other local provenance seeds deposited there so far included red hemp nettle (from finds at just three sites), shepherd's needle (which had been found at two sites), night-flowering catchfly and large-flowered hemp nettle.

The project became a national showcase for the restoration of arable plants and was recognised by Natural England as a Nationally Significant Project. With only one paid officer, much of the work was still done by volunteers, with the support of local farmers and many organisations: the Country Landowners Association, National Farmers Union, Farming and Wildlife Advisory Group, Central Science Laboratory (now the Food and Environment Research Agency), DEFRA, Howardian Hills AONB, Ryedale District Council, Scarborough Borough Council and North Yorkshire County Council. School visits to the field at RFM proved very popular and enabled children to learn about traditional farming methods. Farmers also benefited, as they were given help to access agri-environment grants.

As the project expanded, local botanists were trained to recognise the rare species and to join in the project. Talks were given to local organisations and promotional leaflets produced. Media coverage included farming journals, local radio, local and national television and printed news media. The project had stands at agricultural shows, biodiversity fairs and a Yorkshire Naturalists' Union conference. At RFM, special events and annual harvest days were held each year, and the project even received a royal visit from Prince Andrew! A high quality photographic exhibition was produced and a book about the project published, *A Harvest of Colour*, written by Ian Carstairs.

After such a success story, it was expected that the work would harmonise with Environmental Stewardship schemes as part of the mainstream Natural England work. However, these schemes turned out to be too blunt and inflexible in the early stages. Another major leap forward was therefore required.

Phase 3: out of intensive care

The next phase of the project, which began in 2010, will take the work to a wider audience and establish a stand-alone group to take the project forward into the future. Funding for a further five years has been acquired from the National Park's Sustainable Development Fund, the North York Moors Coast and Hills LEADER Programme and the Heritage Lottery Fund. The North Yorkshire Moors Association joined the three original partner bodies, and a second part-time project officer, Tom Normandale, has been appointed to work alongside Chris Wilson. Management of the core sites will continue at Silpho, the RFM and the Mushroom Field, Spaunton (NYMNPA management agreement site), although the original cornfield at the RFM will be rested in 2012. As well as the many farmers' fields involved in the project, disused chalk and limestone quarries will also be used, as many cornfield flowers survive well in these sites. It is also hoped to involve small-scale farmers and non-farming landowners, to create more sites for re-establishing species.

Fieldwork to locate new sites of surviving arable plants will continue. More gardeners will be recruited to expand the seed stock and engage the wider public in the conservation work. School children will also be used to help harvest the seeds and grow on some of the plants. The project has the potential for extending expertise into the cultivation of other plants that are threatened in the wild, and to deposit more seeds with the Millennium Seed Bank.

Conclusion: the future

It is by no means certain that funding will continue after the next few years, so it is essential that the project should become self-sustaining by 2015. The intention is to set up a dedicated group of volunteers who can take over from the paid staff, offering advice and demonstrations to farmers and continuing to educate the public about the conservation of arable plants. This project has illustrated how a group of plants near extinction in the wild has been brought 'back from the edge'. It is hoped that a long-term, secure future will be obtained for our cornfield flowers, as a cherished and valuable part of the agricultural landscape.

Reference

Carstairs, I. (2006) *A Harvest of Colour.* Halsgrove Publishing, Wellington, Somerset.

Times they are a changing...........looking back to the future for Yorkshire's wildlife

Ian D. Rotherham
Sheffield Hallam University

Figure 1. Female Banded Demoiselle on the River Rother by Ian Rotherham

Introduction
We held the Sheffield-based conference in 2013 which was in the shadow of the major economic downturn and the punitive cuts to public services including nature conservation. However, spurred on in part by the 2010 Lawton Report many conservation organisations (mostly NGOs) have endeavoured to deliver a vision which is 'bigger, better, bolder, more joined'. Remarkable successes have been achieved despite the dwindling support from agencies and from local governmental sources.

In the uplands great strides have been made to block the historic grips that drained the moors and bogs and even to reintroduce sphagnum mosses to help reconstruct a functioning upland ecosystem. Clearly though it will take many decades at least to fully restore the damaged peatlands and indeed, full functionality may not be possible. The upland meadows and roadside verges may be more difficult to maintain or to restore and with them lies the fate of birds like the Twite. There is little sign of any meaningful recovery as yet. Similarly the issues of illegal persecution of upland birds of prey such as the iconic Hen Harrier hangs like a dark shadow over some moorland estates. Great progress has been made with some moorland owners but for others it will take a long time for their reputations to be fully recovered.

Also in the uplands, the increasingly widespread use of moorlands and bogs for intensive, active recreation, particularly with massed night-time groups of mountain-bikers with high-impact lighting must surely have impacts on mammal and bird fauna. The damage to vegetation and erosion of footpaths and even archaeological sites is clear to see. Whilst we welcome increased public participation in outdoor leisure activities, everything has its place, and that includes nature.

Lowland areas remain under pressure from intensive agriculture on the one hand, and sprawling urbanisation on the other. Some of the lowland farming areas will need to adapt as climate charge and sea level rise combine with the wind-erosion of former peatland 'bread-basket' soils to create a perfect storm of increasingly unfavourable conditions. Farming will need to adapt and to do so significantly within the next fifty years. In this context, the loss of the 'Yorkshire Farming and Wildlife Advisory Group' as both an advocate and a source of expert guidance must be regarded as a huge dent in our ability to change. This is even more concerning when with Brexit looming there are such big decisions to be made. The interface between farmers and nature conservation becomes increasingly critical to society's potential to adapt.

There are major projects such as the massive restoration of the Humberhead Levels and the wetland outliers such as Potteric Carr. Nevertheless, despite the large scale of these projects, they only address the core sites and not the wider context of the bigger landscape. Arguments such as the sequestration of carbon into restored peatlands may trigger some policy-level responses to opportunities such as Thorne and Hatfield Moors in the lowlands, and Moors for the Future in the uplands. However, realistically whilst the successes must be welcomed, the challenge extends way beyond these core sites. Across huge landscapes of former peatlands that are now drained and in intensive agricultural usage, there is still far more peat-carbon being released than that mopped up by the targeted conservation schemes; yet nobody talks about this haemorrhaging of soil carbon and its potential impacts on climate. Al Gore would describe this as an 'inconvenient truth'.

Large nature reserve projects such as RSPB Old Moor in the Dearne Valley, and Potteric Carr in Doncaster, have brought back birds such as breeding Bitterns, Mediterranean Gull, Avocet, and more. This is wonderful news and furthermore, large numbers of people now enjoy the wildlife spectaculars and their tourism spending is helping to restore damaged local economies in former industrial areas.

Figure 2. Kingfisher by Brent Hardy

Great steps have been made to both clean up and restructure damaged rivers across the county though more remains to be done. Formerly dead rivers such as the Dearne, Don and Rother now boast good numbers of fish including trout, salmon, and maybe fifteen or more other species. Otters have returned in good numbers though Water Voles remain under threat. Birds such as Kingfisher, Grey Heron, Cormorant, and Goosander are now seen along most watercourses. With cleaner water and restored riverside habitats the Environment Agency and their partners have reintroduced fish-stocks and even the necessary waterweed required for them to thrive. Along rivers like the Rother and Don, in with the waterweed were numbers of insects such as the Banded Demoiselle damselflies. These are now seen all along these watercourses as an aquatic rewilding of often unfavourable urban and rural habitats. Less good has been the deliberate introduction to the region's catchments of the North American Signal Crayfish and the eradication of the native Crayfish. The relevant authorities knew what was happening but the increasingly emasculated conservation agencies seemed incapable of responding or even implementing what little conservation legislation exists.

Figure 3. Signal Crayfish by Ian Rotherham

Water remains hugely significant across the county with periodic inundations wreaking havoc with floods in York on a regular basis, in cities like Leeds and Sheffield, and in towns around the Pennines like Hebden Bridge and Holmfirth. Lowland settlements and coastal cities such as Hull in particular, are increasingly under threat from inland floods and coastal surges. The winter of 2013 was especially notable for catastrophic surges along the East Coast; and here too, there is the on-going threat of accelerating coastal erosion which again no politicians or planners are willing to address.

The 'Meccas' for Yorkshire seabirds of Flamborough and Bempton especially, are still thriving but there are continuing threats of climate–induced shifts in the fish on which the great seabird colonies depend. So even here, the future for some species is far from certain. However, along the Yorkshire coastline there are attempts to enhance natural habitat and to grow wildlife-related tourism. Yorkshire Wildlife Trust and the RSPB have been leading the way; although when, back in the 1990s and early 2000s, I first advocated the potential importance of this for the regional economy, it felt like nobody was listening.

Across the county the Wildlife Trusts, the RSPB, the Woodland Trust, the National Trust and a myriad local groups are working hard for Yorkshire's natural heritage. In some cases the results are astounding. To look up and see Peregrine Falcons, Common Buzzards, and Red Kites overhead is wonderful; for this to be in Sheffield city centre is remarkable. However, especially in towns and cities, but across the wider landscape too, there are other changes afoot. Triggered in part by fluxing climate, by other environmental changes, and by accidental escapes or deliberate introductions, our Yorkshire wildlife and its ecology are hybridising to form what is called a 'recombinant ecology'. Some conservation efforts are at least slowing the spread of non-native animals and plants, but they are not halting them. Hybrid ecologies now exist in many places across the county from the urban River Don with its wild Fig Trees, Japanese Knotweed, Himalayan Balsam, and North American Mink, to the centre of York with its feral Grey Lag and Canada Geese. Wild Buddleia now spreads through every urban area and increasingly in the rural landscape too. The list goes on, and the process was to some extent forecast in the 1990s by George Barker for English Nature and by the late Oliver Gilbert in his pioneering works on urban habitats. You may not like the prospect but be reassured, Yorkshire's wildlife future is a hybrid one!

113

References

Lawton, Sir J. (2010) *'Making Space for Nature': a review of England's Wildlife Sites and Ecological Network.* Department for Environment Food & Rural Affairs, London.

Rotherham I.D. (2017a) *Shadow Woods: A Search for Lost Landscapes.* Wildtrack Publishing, Sheffield.

Rotherham, I.D. (2017b) *Recombinant Ecology – a hybrid future?* Springer Briefs, Springer, Dordrecht.

Rotherham, I.D. (2017c) *The Industrial Transformation of South Yorkshire Landscapes.* **In:** Rotherham, I.D., & Handley, C. (eds) (2017) *The Industrial Legacy & Landscapes of Sheffield and South Yorkshire.* Wildtrack Publishing, Sheffield, 3 - 40.

Rotherham, I.D. (2017d*) Eco-fusion of alien and native as a new conceptual framework for historical ecology.* In: Vaz, E., de Melo, C.J., & Pinto, L. (eds) *Environmental history in the making. Volume1*, Springer, Dordrecht, The Netherlands, 73 - 90.

Rotherham, I.D. (2015a) Bio-Cultural Heritage & Biodiversity - emerging paradigms in conservation and planning. *Biodiversity & Conservation*, 24, 3405-3429.

Rotherham, I.D. (2015b) Times they are a changin' – Recombinant Ecology as an emerging paradigm. *International Urban Ecology Review*, 5, 1-19.

Rotherham, I.D. (2015c) Relict communities and urban commons – urban distinctiveness, history and sustainable urban diversity. *International Urban Ecology Review*, 5, 29-38.

For

South Yorkshire Biodiversity Research Group

(www.ukeconet.org)

&

PLACE

**People, Landscape & Cultural Environment
Education and Research Centre**

place@yorksj.ac.uk

www.place.uk.com

2|23| - |J.R.